CNN® Guide

to the 1992 Election

Change vs. Trust

THOMAS B. ALLEN

Turner Publishing, Inc.

ATLANTA

PUBLISHED BY TURNER PUBLISHING, INC.

A SUBSIDIARY OF TURNER BROADCASTING SYSTEM, INC.

ONE CNN CENTER, BOX 105366

ATLANTA, GEORGIA 30348-5366

FIRST EDITION 10 9 8 7 6 5 4 3 2 1

THOMAS B. ALLEN

CNN GUIDE TO THE 1992 ELECTION

LIBRARY OF CONGRESS CATALOG CARD NUMBER: 92-64120

SOFTCOVER ISBN: 1-878685-25-2

DISTRIBUTED BY ANDREWS AND MCMEEL

4900 MAIN STREET

KANSAS CITY, MISSOURI 64112

DESIGNED AND PRODUCED ON MACINTOSH COMPUTERS USING QUARKXPRESS,
ALDUS FREEHAND, AND ADOBE PHOTOSHOP. COLOR SEPARATIONS AND
FILM PREPARATION BY GRAPHICS INTERNATIONAL, ATLANTA, GEORGIA.
PRINTING BY RINGIER AMERICA, NEW BERLIN, WISCONSIN.

EDITORIAL: ALAN SCHWARTZ, EDITOR-IN-CHIEF

KATHERINE BUTTLER, ASSISTANT EDITOR

MARIAN LORD, COPY EDITOR

JAMES PORGES, RESEARCH COORDINATOR

DESIGN: MICHAEL WALSH, DESIGN DIRECTOR

ELAINE STREITHOF, DESIGN/PRODUCTION

KAREN SMITH, DESIGN/PRODUCTION

NANCY ROBINS, PRODUCTION DIRECTOR

KEN MOWRY, INFORMATIONAL GRAPHICS

MARTY MOORE, PHOTO AND VIDEO RESEARCH

MAUREEN PIERCE, VIDEO RESEARCH

ELIZABETH AZAR, VIDEO RESEARCH

J. STOLL, PHOTO AND VIDEO RESEARCH

Turner

Table of Contents

ELECTION '92

IN THE SUMMER OF 1991, CNN began final planning for its coverage of the political campaign and election. At the time it seemed that covering the 1992 presidential race would be dull. President Bush had piled up spectacular polls during the Persian Gulf war, and it appeared that the Democrats would be left with selecting a sacrificial lamb at best.

But, much changed throughout the next 12 months: the rise and fall of Senator Paul Tsongas, the character issue surrounding Governor Bill Clinton and his ability to withstand microscopic scrutiny, the surprising early showing of Pat Buchanan, the spectacular ascent and non-candidacy of Ross Perot, the impact of former Governor Jerry Brown and his unconventional candidacy, the controversy surrounding Vice President Dan Quayle's remaining on the Republican ticket, and President Bush falling from an 89 percent approval rating to a 22-point underdog position, then rebounding after the Republican convention.

Abortion, jobs, the economy, U.S. Supreme Court appointments, aid to Russia, the continuing menace of Saddam Hussein, all added to the political fray.

The saga of Campaign '92—that is what this book is designed to capture...and more. To guide viewers and voters through the images and issues as America selects a President for the next four years. From the first moments of the campaign, into the primaries and the conventions, to the formal start of the fall election drive, this book provides voters with information to make decisions thoughtfully.

None of us knows what the final weeks of this tumultuous political season will bring. We do know the *CNN Guide to the 1992 Election* is an exciting history of what has happened and a road map, at least, for the days ahead.

TOM JOHNSON *President, CNN*

CHANGE VS.

TRUST

O N APRIL 29 SIRENS and gunfire drowned out the words of the presidential campaign. A jury without blacks had just acquitted four white Los Angeles police officers who had been videotaped beating Rodney G. King, a black man. Blacks and Hispanics in Los Angeles reacted with fury, burning and plundering and triggering the worst riots America has seen in this century.

For the candidates, the real issues spilled out on mean streets. Urban policy? Here was a city going up in flames. Racial issues? Here were Korean merchants shooting at blacks and Hispanics. Poverty statistics? Here were the people without jobs, without hope. Crime issues? Here were looters and killers. A 15-year-old black student killed by a random shot as he stood on his lawn. A 68-year-old white man strangled by looters. A 65-year-old Latino woman shot to death as she walked down her street.

Clinton arrived in Los Angeles after a string of primary victories had made him the almost certain Democratic presidential nominee. At a time and place that demanded eloquence, he spoke in platitudes: "The key to any long-term progress is the economic and political empowerment of the people who are most disadvantaged."

Bush spoke from a lectern in the Mount Zion Missionary Baptist

South-central Los Angeles burns as racial rioting erupts in April.

Church in south-central Los Angeles, the heart of the riot zone. He looked up from his written notes and, his voice choking, said, "We should take nothing but sorrow out of all of that"—more than 50 people dead, thousands of small businesses burned to the ground. "I pray to God that He will give us the strength and the wisdom to bring the family together, the American family."

The American family of four, as defined in 1990 by the U.S. government, was in poverty if it had an income of $13,359 or less. The 1990 U.S. census showed that the number of people in official poverty had increased by 4.3 million between 1979 and 1989. About 25 percent of the people in poverty were children under 18. The poverty rate among blacks living in American cities like Los Angeles rose from 21.2 percent in 1969 to 33.8 percent in 1990, while the white inner-city poverty rate was 14.4 percent. Statistics predicted that 97 of every 100 white children in that poverty might escape; of 100 black children, 66 might escape.

When Clinton was nominated and George Bush was about to be, a CNN/USA *Today*/Gallup Poll showed that 84 percent of the Americans surveyed were dissatisfied with the state of the nation. That was the highest level of discontent since 1979, when President Jimmy Carter said the nation was suffering a "crisis in confidence."

From New England to California, unemployment kept rising. The recession dragged on. The mountainous budget deficit steadily grew. Personal bankruptcies soared. Employers were laying off thousands of workers who had thought their jobs would last to retirement. And retirement was only a dream for many; the percentage of workers with employer pension plans dropped from 61 in 1979 to 55 percent in 1992.

The voters were demanding change, but no change seemed in sight.

During George Bush's inaugural address on January 20, 1989, he turned to Democratic congressional leaders seated on the platform and reached his hand out to them. "The American people await action," he said. "They didn't send us here to bicker."

Thus began the Bush years. In the very first moments of his presidency George Bush dramatized what he faced: a divided government. Richard Nixon had endured it. He was the first elected President in the 20th Century to enter office with both houses of Congress controlled by the opposition party. Bush confronted the same obstacle, grown bigger. The election that brought in Bush also brought in an 85-seat Democratic majority in the House—the most formidable opposition ever faced by a new President.

At the beginning, Bush did not worry about Congress. As he made the smooth transition from President Ronald Reagan's Vice President to Reagan's successor, nothing on the horizon threatened Bush or his nation. Soviet troops were withdrawing from Afghanistan, Eastern Europe was turning away from communism, and the Soviet Union was too distracted by internal politics to try any foreign adventures.

Domestically, he was saddled with Reagan's budget, which projected a deficit of $91.1 billion, narrowly below the statutory Gramm-Rudman limit of $100 billion. The Congressional Budget Office predicted that the deficit for fiscal 1990 would be substantially higher than Reagan had estimated. Tax increases would ease the budget burden, but, in those early days of the Bush Administration, no tax increase was in sight.

Bush had also inherited the collapse of the savings and loan industry. He proposed to deal with the crisis by closing or selling off 350 S&Ls and revamping the federal regulating system. The launching of this rescue plan would initially cost $157.6 billion, with the taxpayers and the thrift industry splitting the bill.

Because of the economic restraints imposed by the deficit and his no-new-taxes pledge, Bush could not introduce any expensive programs. But, recalling his campaign promise to be the "Education President," he proposed a $444 million plan aimed at improving educational quality. Democrats dismissed the Bush education initiative as inadequate. Such partisan bickering dogged his every legislative move.

As Bush began his term, a Gallup poll showed that 56 percent of the American people were satisfied with the way things were going in the United States, compared with only 17 percent who felt that way when President Reagan entered the White House in 1981. In the same poll, 87 percent of the people interviewed said they were satisfied with the state of their personal lives. That was the highest rating since Gallup first asked about personal satisfaction in 1979.

What Bush did not realize was that approval over how he did his job was linked to a growing public distaste for Congress and gridlock. As squabbles between the President and the Congress escalated to sustained conflict, the voters, like innocents caught in a crossfire, began damning both sides.

On October 2, 1990, Bush asked the people to call on the Congress to support a compromise budget agreement that included a tax increase. He warned that "if we fail to enact this agreement, our economy will falter, markets may tumble, and recession will follow." The plan contained $134 billion in tax increases. Bush's plea did no good. The House rejected the plan, 254 to 179, with 105 out of 176 House Republicans among those voting no. The government was technically penniless. On October 6, the Statue of Liberty, the Smithsonian, and other national monuments and museums shut down. Finally came a budget agreement that included increases in the high-tax bracket and a cut in the capital-gains tax that Bush had long wanted. On October 27, the "deficit-reduction" compromise was enacted and signed into law.

Since June, when Bush said he would have to break his pledge on taxes, voters had been seething. They would get their chance to react in the November congressional elections. Wholesale eviction of incumbents was forecast. But the voters' revolt did not erupt. In August, Iraq had invaded Kuwait, the United States had begun sending troops to Saudi Arabia, and Americans had rallied behind the President.

By election day, voters had forgotten, or at least had put aside, their anger over the tax increase. But they did cast more ballots for Democrats than for Republicans. Enough Democratic governors won to put a Democratic slant on reapportionment decisions that would come in the wake of the 1990 census.

The startling portrait of America revealed by that census began to emerge in 1991. Here were the indelible figures of change, the statistics that reflected an America vastly different from the one that Bush had known when he became Ronald Reagan's Vice President. Within the statistical portrait could be seen many more children struggling with poverty, and immigrants thwarted as they sought the American dream.

Between June 1990 and December 1991, more than 3 million jobs disappeared. With individual incomes of young families falling, both husband and wife had to work. Traditionally, mothers of children under three once did not make up much of the labor force. Now about 55 percent of them were looking for jobs—about the same percentage as all married women. Families were changing, America was changing.

The world—the summit-conference, treaty-signing, world of President Bush and Secretary of State James Baker—was also changing, and they were agents of that change. But, aloft in Air Force One or secluded in the Oval Office, Bush did not seem to notice the changes in the nation he governed.

In February 1992, two days after the New Hampshire primary, a CNN/*Time* telephone poll asked 1,250 American adults, "Does Bush understand the problems of the average American?" Fifty-nine percent of them said he did not.

Baker, the man Bush trusted the most, was no longer watching the polls or jawing with the state chairmen. He was a statesman now, a man concerned more with the Middle East than the Middle West. Bush would need Baker for counsel, but the realization of that need would come only after the riots, after Bush's approval ratings dropped, after Bill Clinton had been nominated and had found his campaign theme: "It's time for a change in America."

The idea of change catapulted Ross Perot into the campaign, and when he withdrew, both Clinton and Bush reached out to his dismayed supporters. Bush had already tried to seize the change theme. By one count, in seven appearances in April alone he mentioned change or reform 188 times.

But by now Jim Baker had come to Bush's aid. The election, Baker said, is not about change. It is about trust. And so, when Bush accepted renomination in August, he said the question that must be answered in this election is: "Who do you trust to make change work for you?"

"Trust" replaces "change" in Bush speeches—and in Bush cartoons.

Lech Walesa
Solidarity Leader

APRIL 5, 1989

JANUARY 20, 1989   **MAY 4, 1989**

Countdown to Election '92

The events, at home and abroad, that paced the Bush presidency

1 9 8 9

JAN 20: George Bush inaugurated as 41st President.

FEB 6: Bush proposes plan to close or sell 350 ailing savings and loans.

FEB 9: Bush unveils $1.16 trillion budget, with a projected deficit of $91.1 billion.

FEB 15: Soviet Union says all troops are out of Afghanistan.

MARCH 24: The oil tanker 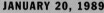 Exxon Valdez runs aground in the Gulf of Alaska and spills 240,000 barrels of oil, the largest such ecological disaster in U.S. history.

MARCH 26: In the Soviet Union's first multi-party parliamentary elections since 1917, reform leader Boris Yeltsin wins seat, as many Communist Party candidates lose.

APRIL 5: Polish Communist leaders agree to free elections and legalization of Solidarity.

APRIL 17: House Ethics Committee accuses House Speaker Jim Wright, a Texas Democrat, of 69 ethics violations.

APRIL 25: Defense Department Secretary Cheney proposes $10 billion cuts for fiscal 1990. Democrats start talking about "peace dividend."

MAY 4: 100,000 pro-democracy Chinese students and workers march in Beijing to demand democratic reforms.

Marine Lt. Col. Oliver North found guilty on 3 of 12 counts in Iran-Contra trial.

MAY 10: Bush denounces "massive irregularities" in Panama presidential election, calls on Noriega to resign, and increases U.S. military forces in Panama.

MAY 18: Congress adopts compromise $1.2 trillion budget.

MAY 18: Legislatures in Soviet Baltic states of Estonia and Lithuania declare independence.

JUNE 3-4: Chinese army troops and tanks crush student-led pro-democracy protests in Beijing's Tiananmen Square, killing hundreds, possibly thousands. Bush announces sanctions against the Chinese government.

JUNE 3-4, 1989

JULY 3, 1989

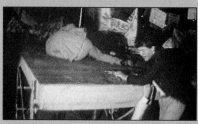

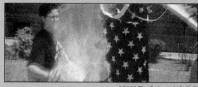

JUNE 21, 1989

AUGUST 18, 1989

Iran's Ayatollah Khomeini dies; Ali Khamenei chosen as President.

JUNE 6: Democrat Thomas S. Foley of Washington State elected Speaker of House.

JUNE 12: Supreme Court rules that white workers claiming unfair treatment because of affirmative action programs can seek amends under civil rights laws.

JUNE 13: Bush vetoes bill to increase minimum wage; the House sustains veto.

JUNE 15: House legislation authorizes $157 billion bailout of S&Ls.

JUNE 21: Supreme Court says flag burning is protected by First Amendment. One week later, Bush calls for constitutional amendment to protect U.S. flag.

JUNE 28-JULY 11: Chinese leadership steps up attacks on pro-democracy movement. U.S. House votes sanctions against China.

JULY 3: Supreme Court upholds Missouri abortion restrictions in what is seen as prelude to overruling Roe v. Wade decision that legalized abortion.

JULY 11: HUD Secretary Kemp estimates that HUD lost $2 billion in fraud and waste under Reagan Administration.

JULY 17-18: At Geneva disarmament talks, the United States and the Soviet Union agree on ban of chemical weapons.

JULY 26: Slowing economic growth indicates U.S. economy may be headed for recession.

AUG 9: Bush signs thrift industry bailout law that provides $166 billion over 10 years to close or merge insolvent thrifts. Taxpayers will pick up three-quarters of the bill.

AUG 17: Polish President Gen. Wojciech Jaruzelski approves Solidarity-led coalition government.

AUG 18: Colombian Liberal Party presidential candidate Luis Carlos Galan assassinated by Medellin cartel drug lords.

SEPT 6: South Africa's ruling National Party is weakened by white parliamentary election. NP leader De Klerk sees vote as mandate to proceed with gradual reform of the apartheid system.

SEPT 11-14 : More than 13,000 East Germans who had entered Hungary emigrate to West Germany via Austria. East Germany demands that Hungary halt the exodus.

SEPT 21: Vietnam completes withdrawal of troops from Cambodia.

SEPT 26: In a national poll, Bush gets higher approval rating than any of his four predecessors at this point in their terms.

DECEMBER 20, 1989

NOVEMBER 9, 1989

DECEMBER 29, 1989

SEPT 30-OCT 4 : More than 17,000 East Germans emigrate to West Germany from Poland and Czechoslovakia.

OCT 11: House votes to restore Medicaid funds to pay for abortion in cases of rape or incest.

OCT 12: NASA reports "ozone hole" in the Arctic.

OCT 21: Bush vetoes bill that contains proviso for Medicaid payments for abortions in cases of rape or incest.

OCT 23: Hungary proclaims itself a free republic.

OCT 28: Some 10,000 pro-democracy demonstrators protest in Prague.

NOV 7: Lt. Gov. L. Douglas Wilder of Virginia, a Democrat, is elected the nation's first black governor.

NOV 9: East Germany opens the Berlin Wall.

NOV 24: Bowing to the pro-democracy movement, Czechoslovakia' Communist Party leaders resign.

DEC 2-3: Leadership of East Germany's Communist Party resigns; Party Secretary Erich Honecher arrested.

DEC 19: West German Chancellor Helmut Kohl visits East Germany and begins

process of reunification.

DEC 20: U.S. forces invade Panama. Noriega eludes capture. New government is sworn in.

DEC 25: Romanian President Nicholas Ceausescu and his wife are executed by military firing squad after 10 days of growing pro-democracy protests and an army revolt.

DEC 29: For the first time in 40 years a non-Communist, playwright Vaclav Havel, is elected president of Czechoslovakia.

1 9 9 0

JAN 5: Iraqi leader Saddam Hussein offers peace proposal to end the Iran-Iraq War.

JAN 10: Chinese Premier Li Peng lifts martial law; Tiananmen Square, scene of bloody suppression of pro-democracy demonstrations, reopens.

JAN 16: In Tampa, Fla., officials of Luxembourg-based Bank of Credit & Commerce International Holdings (BCCI) plead guilty to money laundering.

JAN 18: National poll shows Bush, after one year in office, has highest approval rating of any President since World War II, at this point in the term.

JAN 22: Kuwaiti police, using tear gas,

FEBRUARY 25, 1990

FEBRUARY 11, 1990

MARCH 11, 1990

water cannons, and stun grenades, break up pro-democracy demonstration.

JAN 29: Bush sends to Congress a $1.23 trillion budget that does not raise taxes and abides by federal deficit ceiling, with slight cuts in defense spending and larger cuts in many domestic programs.

JAN 31: In State of the Union address Bush proposes a mutual U.S.-Soviet reduction of forces in central Europe to 195,000 each. Bush praises Gov. Bill Clinton of Arkansas and three other governors for their work in Bush's "education summit" in fall 1990.

FEB 7: In victory for Gorbachev, Soviet Communist Party Central Committee renounces constitutionally guaranteed monopoly on political power.

FEB 11: South African black nationalist leader Nelson Mandela freed after 27 years in jail.

FEB 11-13: Foreign ministers of NATO and Warsaw Pact agree on German reunification.

FEB 25: Violeta Chamorro of National Opposition Union defeats Sandinistas in Nicaraguan national elections.

FEB 28: Reports surface of fraud at Atlanta branch of Banca Nazionale del Lavoro, Italy's largest state-owned bank. Democratic Representative Henry Gonzalez

of Texas, chairman of the House Banking Committee, says his probe into BNL was facing "substantial and formidable obstruction" by the Federal Reserve and the Justice Department under the guise of protecting "national Security."

MARCH 6: Senate confirms Clarence Thomas for seat on U.S. Circuit Court of Appeals for District of Columbia.

MARCH 11: Lithuanian Supreme Soviet declares republic's independence from Soviet Union.

MARCH 13-15: Soviet Congress revokes Communist Party political monopoly, elects Gorbachev to five-year term as president.

MARCH 15: Fernando Collor de Mello becomes first democratically elected president of Brazil in 30 years.

MARCH 17-22: After Lithuanian parliament forms non-Communist coalition government, Soviet military forces threaten Lithuanian capital of Vilnius.

MARCH 26: New U.S. Office of Thrift Supervision reports that America's thrift industry lost $19.7 billion in 1989.

APRIL 7: Federal jury convicts retired Vice Adm. John Poindexter, former Reagan Administration national security adviser, on five felony counts for his involvement in the Iran-Contra scandal.

APRIL 24, 1990

JUNE 1, 1990   **JUNE 22, 1990 >**

APRIL 24: Drexel Burnham Lambert's Michael Milken pleads guilty to securities fraud, agrees to pay $600 million in fines and restitution.

MAY 2-4: African National Congress and South African government begin talks that will lead to a new constitution giving equal status to blacks.

MAY 9: Bush opposes UN plan for providing direct aid to Third World countries to reduce use of ozone-depleting chlorofluorocarbons.

MAY 23: Testifying before congressional committee, Neil Bush, son of the President, denies wrongdoing as director of failed Denver S&L.

MAY 24: Bush, ignoring congressional critics, recommends renewal of most-favored-nation trade status for China.

MAY 27: Ethnic violence breaks out in Soviet republics of Armenia and Kirghizia.

MAY 29: Boris Yeltsin elected president of Russian Federation.

JUNE 1: Bush and Gorbachev sign agreement to reduce strategic nuclear weapons.

JUNE 7: World Resources Institute study says rain forests are vanishing 50% faster than predicted.

JUNE 11: Supreme Court strikes down 1989 federal law forbidding desecration of the American flag.

Poindexter sentenced to six-month prison term for lying to Congress about his involvement in Iran-Contra scandal.

JUNE 15: In a policy reversal, Bush backs "ozone-layer fund" for developing countries.

JUNE 22: Northern spotted owl declared endangered species; Pacific northwest loggers protest.

JUNE 26: Bush moves to delay spotted owl protection plan.

JULY 16: Soviets say they will allow a reunified Germany to join NATO.

JULY 18: Iraq's Saddam Hussein threatens force against Kuwait and the United Arab Emirates to keep them from driving down oil prices by overproduction.

JULY 20: U.S. Court of Appeals suspends Oliver North's three felony convictions in Iran-Contra and overturns one.

JULY 23: Iraqi troops reported massing on Kuwaiti border.

AUG 2: Iraqi forces invade Kuwait. The United States calls invasion "naked aggression."

Saudi Arabia

AUGUST 22, 1990

CNN LIVE

OCTOBER 2, 1990

AUG 6: UN Security Council votes to impose trade embargo on Iraq. Bush sends U.S. military forces to Saudi Arabia to defend oil fields.

AUG 8-16: Egypt and other Arab nations dispatch troops to join U.S. forces in Saudi Arabia. Saddam urges holy war.

AUG 22: Bush calls up reserves for Gulf action, dubbed Operation Desert Shield.

AUG 23: Armenia declares independence from Soviet Union.

SEPT 11: Bush vows defeat of Iraqis.

SEPT 12: World War II allies formally end responsibilities over Germany in key step toward reunification.

SEPT 13: Hearings open on David H. Souter, federal Appeals Court judge from New Hampshire, nominated for Supreme Court.

SEPT 16: France, Britain send troops to Saudi Arabia, as do Argentina, Canada, and Italy.

SEPT 18: Charles Keating, former head of plundered S&L, indicted on criminal fraud charges.

SEPT 21: Saddam Hussein warns Iraqis to prepare for "mother of all battles."

Federal Deposit Insurance Corporation, a

federal agency, files $200 million civil suit against Neil Bush and other directors of failed Silverado S&L.

SEPT 25: UN votes to extend blockade of Iraq.

OCT 2: David Souter becomes Bush's first appointment to the Supreme Court.

OCT 3: Germany reunited.

OCT 5: Cincinnati gallery acquitted of obscenity charge for displaying an exhibit of photographs by late artist Robert Mapplethorpe.

OCT 16: National poll shows Bush's approval rating dropping.

OCT 18: Bush signs expansion of Head Start program, carrying out campaign promise.

OCT 22: Bush vetoes Civil Rights Act of 1990.

OCT 27: After delay, Congress passes "deficit-reduction" act after Bush breaks his "no new taxes" campaign pledge. The bill would raise taxes by $164.4 billion over five years.

NOV 6: Secret CIA report says Iraq is using BNL branch in Atlanta to buy "military-related technology" with U.S.-guaranteed loans supposedly for grain purchases.

NOVEMBER 15, 1990　　　　　　　　**NOVEMBER 22, 1990**

NOV 15: Bush signs first Clean Air Act since 1970.

NOV 21: 34 countries sign treaty ending Cold War.

NOV 22: British Prime Minister Margaret Thatcher resigns after 11 years. John Major succeeds her.

NOV 26: Matsushita Electric Industry of Japan buys the U.S. entertainment conglomerate MCA Inc. for $6.59 billion in the largest acquisition of a U.S. company by Japanese.

DEC 16: Haiti holds first democratic elections.

DEC 18: The Federal Reserve Board votes to cut discount rate for the first time since 1986.

DEC 21: Michael Milken gets ten-year prison sentence for illegal trading activities.

DEC 31: The Dow Jones Industrial Average closes the year at 2633.66, lowest since 1981.

1　9　9　1

JAN 6: Bank of New England files for bankruptcy in the third largest bank failure in U.S. history.

JAN 8: Pan American World Airways files for bankruptcy.

JAN 17: U.S. planes bomb military and weapon-making facilities in Iraq. Operation Desert Storm begins. Bush foresees victory producing "new world order."

Iraq fires Scud missiles at Israel in hopes Israel will be drawn into war, driving out Arab nations. Israel does not retaliate.

JAN 18: Eastern Airlines stops all flights and begins liquidating its assets.

Feb 1: President De Klerk of South Africa repeals last of laws codifying apartheid.

FEB 4: Defense Secretary Cheney announces six-year plan to reduce U.S. military by about 25%.

Bush submits $1.446 trillion budget, projecting a deficit of $280.9 billion.

FEB 12: President's Council of Economic Advisers, responding to rising unemployment rate (6.2) and a loss of 232,000 jobs in January, predicts recession will soon end.

FEB 20: Bush proposes opening the Arctic National Wildlife Refuge and coastal areas of California and Gulf of Mexico to oil exploration.

FEBRUARY 22, 1991

FEBRUARY 24, 1991

MARCH 14, 1991

FEB 22: Bush gives Iraq deadline to pull out of Kuwait or face ground war. Iraqis set fire to Kuwaiti oil installations; half the country under pall of smoke.

FEB 24: At dawn, 200,000 allied troops begin ground offensive that routs Iraqi defenders in 100 hours. Bush stops offensive with thousands of Iraqi forces unscathed. Saddam Hussein remains in power.

FEB 27: Senate Ethics Committee finds evidence of misconduct by Democratic Senator Alan Cranston of California.

MARCH 14: Four white Los Angeles police officers are indicted by a grand jury for beating black motorist Rodney King.

APRIL 3-10: 1 million Kurds flee from Iraq.

APRIL 30: Former U.S. Senator Paul Tsongas enters run for Democratic presidential nomination.

MAY 2: Firefight between Croatians and Serbs in Borovo Selo, Yugoslavia, kills 15 people. Civil war begins.

MAY 4: Bush is treated for irregular heart beat. Physicians trace cause to Graves' Disease. He is pronounced well May 6.

MAY 21: Former Indian Prime Minister Rajiv Gandhi is assassinated.

MAY 23: Supreme Court, in 5-4 decision, upholds federal regulations barring federally funded clinics from providing information about abortion.

JUNE 12: Boris Yeltsin elected president of Russia. Residents of Leningrad vote to change the city's name back to St. Petersburg.

JUNE 25: Slovenia and Croatia declare independence.

JUNE 27: Justice Thurgood Marshall, the first black to sit on the Supreme Court, retires.

JULY 1: Bush nominates Judge Clarence Thomas to U.S. Supreme Court.

JULY 5: Regulators in seven countries begin shut down of the Bank of Credit and Commerce International, alleging systematic fraud.

JULY 9: Ex-CIA official Alan D. Fiers admits lying to Congress regarding Iran-Contra. Scandal imperils the Bush nomination of Robert Gates to become director of the CIA.

JULY 10: Bush Administration lifts U.S. sanctions against South Africa.

JULY 17: Senators quietly vote themselves a pay raise to $125,000, matching the salary of House members.

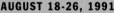

AUGUST 18-26, 1991

OCTOBER 15, 1991

JULY 31: Bush and Gorbachev sign the Strategic Arms Reduction Treaty (START) at a Moscow summit.

AUG 18-26: Communist hardliners try to overthrow Gorbachev. Coup fails; collapse of the USSR begins.

SEPT 5: The Soviet Parliament gives sweeping powers to the republics.

Noriega goes on trial for money laundering and drug trafficking.

SEPT 6: Estonia, Latvia, Lithuania gain independence.

Bush asks Congress to hold up action on $10 billion loan guarantee to Israel in move to pressure Israel from continuing to build settlements in the occupied territories. Bush mentions intense Israeli lobbying, offending U.S. Jewish leaders.

SEPT 15: Senator Tom Harkin of Iowa enters Democratic presidential race.

SEPT 16: Charges against former White House aide Oliver North in Iran-Contra scandal are dismissed.

SEPT 23-24: U.N. experts in Iraq uncover evidence Iraq has nuclear weapons program.

SEPT 26: House leaders announce that House bank would no longer cover

overdrafts. Reports reveal 8,331 bounced checks in 12-month period.

SEPT 30: Military coup removes Haiti's first democratically elected president, Jean-Bertrand Aristide.

Senator Bob Kerrey of Nebraska enters Democratic presidential race.

OCT 1: United States suspends economic aid to Haiti, refuses to recognize military junta.

OCT 3: Gov. Bill Clinton of Arkansas enters Democratic presidential race.

House Speaker Tom Foley announces House bank will close as reports surface that members had $300,000 in unpaid bills at the House restaurant.

OCT 5: Gorbachev announces one-year moratorium on nuclear testing.

OCT 8: Exxon Corp. must pay $1.025 billion in fines and restitution for the Alaskan oil spill.

OCT 9: NASA announces ozone level above Antarctica lowest on record.

OCT 15: Clarence Thomas becomes U.S. Supreme Court Justice after bitter confirmation battle that includes sexual harassment charges made against Thomas by Anita F. Hill, a former aide.

NOVEMBER 12, 1991

OCTOBER 18, 1991　　　　　　　　**DECEMBER 4, 1991**

OCT 18: Republican David Duke, former Ku Klux Klan Grand Wizard, comes in second in Louisiana's gubernatorial primary.

OCT 21: Former California governor, Jerry Brown, enters Democratic presidential race.

OCT 30: Arab-Israeli peace conference, under U.S.-Soviet sponsorship, meets in Madrid. For the first time, all the major parties convene.

U.S., British, and French investigators charge Libyan intelligence officers with plotting the bombing of Pan American World Airways Flight 103.

NOV 6: Firefighters cap last of 700 Kuwaiti oil wells set afire by Iraqi forces.

NOV 12: Robert Gates becomes the director of the CIA; confirmation hearings focused on his role during the Iran-Contra scandal.

NOV 15: Bush, under pressure because of the recession, signs $5.3 billion bill extending benefits for the long-term unemployed.

NOV 16: Ex-KKK leader David Duke loses Louisiana gubernatorial runoff election to former Gov. Edwin W. Edwards.

NOV 19: Bush vetoes congressional attempt to annul "gag rule" that prohibits federal funds to clinics providing information about abortion.

NOV 20: "Keating Five" scandal ends with a reprimand for Democratic Sen. Alan Cranston for aiding former S&L owner Charles H. Keating, Jr.

NOV 21: Bush signs Civil Rights Act.

DEC 3: White House Chief of Staff John H. Sununu resigns after dispute over his use of perks. His departure coincides with sharp decline in Bush performance ratings.

DEC 4: Journalist Terry Anderson, longest held western hostage and last U.S. hostage imprisoned in Lebanon, is freed.

Charles H. Keating, former S&L owner, convicted on fraud charges.

David Duke announces he will run for Republican presidential nomination.

DEC 8: Ukraine, Russia, and Byelorussia sign an agreement to form a Commonwealth of Independent States to replace the USSR.

Kimberly Bergalis, a 23-year-old AIDS victim who had been infected by her dentist, dies.

DEC 10: Ex-Nixon speechwriter and CNN talk-show host Patrick Buchanan announces he will run for Republican presidential nomination.

DEC 19: Bush signs FDIC bailout bill that adds $70 billion to S&L cost.

< **FEBRUARY 20, 1992**   **APRIL 29, 1992**

DEC 20: Prime interest rate drops to lowest level in 14 years—6.5%.

DEC 21: All former Soviet republics but Georgia sign commonwealth agreements.

DEC 25: Gorbachev resigns. Soviet Union officially disbands.

1 9 9 2

JAN 8: Bush, on visit to Japan, collapses at state dinner. He quickly recovers, but televised incident stuns viewers. Bush said trip would aid U.S. auto industry, but critics sense no results.

JAN 11: Military seizes power in Algeria.

JAN 27: Macy's files for bankruptcy.

JAN 29: Bush proposes $1.52 trillion budget.

JAN 31: TWA files for bankruptcy.

FEB 15: Croatia and Slovenia recognized by EEC.

FEB 16: Bush and Chancellor Kohl announce a $24 billion aid package to help Yeltsin carry out reforms.

FEB 20: Texas businessman H. Ross Perot, on a TV talk show, says he will run for President if volunteers put him on ballots in 50 states.

FEB 24: General Motors reports record 1991 loss: $4.45 billion.

MARCH 31: Supreme Court eases restrictions on school desegregation.

APRIL 9: Ex-Panama President Noriega convicted of money laundering and drug trafficking.

APRIL 16: House releases names of current and former members who had overdrafts at House bank.

APRIL 29: Rioting erupts in Los Angeles and elsewhere after jury acquits LA police officers of beating black motorist.

MAY 14: Bush Administration authorizes logging in habitat of endangered spotted owl.

MAY 24: U.S. forces refugees to return to Haiti.

MAY 28, 1992

JUNE 29, 1992

AUGUST 20, 1992

MAY 28: House approves fetal-tissue research.

MAY 30: UN imposes sanctions on Yugoslavia.

JUNE 3-14: Earth Summit in Rio de Janeiro. Bush attends but rejects much of the agenda.

JUNE 11: House Democrats defeat constitutional amendment requiring a balanced budget.

JUNE 16: Bush and Russian President Boris Yeltsin reach agreement on strategic arms reduction.

Former Defense Secretary Casper W. Weinberger indicted in probe of Iran-Contra scandal.

JUNE 17: Yeltsin asks aid for "making the world safe for democracy."

JUNE 23: Israeli Labor Party wins parliamentary election, defeating Shamir government and ushering in government under Yitzhak Rabin.

Bush vetoes bill that would lift ban on use of aborted fetuses in federally funded research.

JUNE 24: Supreme Court rules prayers said at public high school graduation were unconstitutional.

JUNE 26: Navy Secretary H. Lawrence Garrett III resigns in midst of scandal over sexual abuse of women at a naval aviators' convention.

JUNE 29: Supreme Court, in a 5-4 decision, upholds a Pennsylvania law that put limits on abortion. But the court reaffirms a previous decision, Roe v. Wade, which made abortion a basic right.

UN troops take over airport at Sarajevo.

JULY 16: Democrats nominate Arkansas Gov. Bill Clinton for President.

JULY 17: Ross Perot, stunning his volunteer army, withdraws from the race for the presidency.

AUG 20: President George Bush accepts the Republican nomination.

AUG 23: James A. Baker, taking leave as Secretary of State, becomes White House chief of staff to run Bush reelection campaign.

AUG 26: U.S.-led allies declare "no-fly zone" in southern Iraq, to thwart Saddam Hussein's air war against Shiite Muslim rebels.

Bush's Ups & Downs

Percent who approve of the way President Bush is handling his job:

DEC 1989: Panama invasion

AUG 1990: Iraq invades Kuwait

JUNE 1990: Bush drops no-tax pledge

How it looks in August

Presidential preference poll standings taken closest to August of each election year

*1992	George Bush	34%	Bill Clinton	60%	—	—
1988	George Bush	46%	Michael Dukakis	49%	—	—
1984	Ronald Reagan	52%	Walter Mondale	41%	—	—
1980	Ronald Reagan	45%	Jimmy Carter	29%	John Anderson	14%
1976	Gerald Ford	32%	Jimmy Carter	54%	—	—
1972	Richard Nixon	57%	George McGovern	31%	—	—
1968	Richard Nixon	45%	Hubert Humphrey	29%	George Wallace	18%
1964	Barry Goldwater	29%	Lyndon Johnson	65%	—	—
1960	Richard Nixon	50%	John Kennedy	44%	—	—
1956	Dwight Eisenhower	52%	Adlai Stevenson	41%	—	—
1952	Dwight Eisenhower	50%	Adlai Stevenson	43%	—	—
1948	Thomas Dewey	48%	Harry Truman	37%	—	—

SOURCE: The Gallup Poll, Congressional Quarterly, Chicago Tribune

* Prior to Republican Convention

1989　　1990

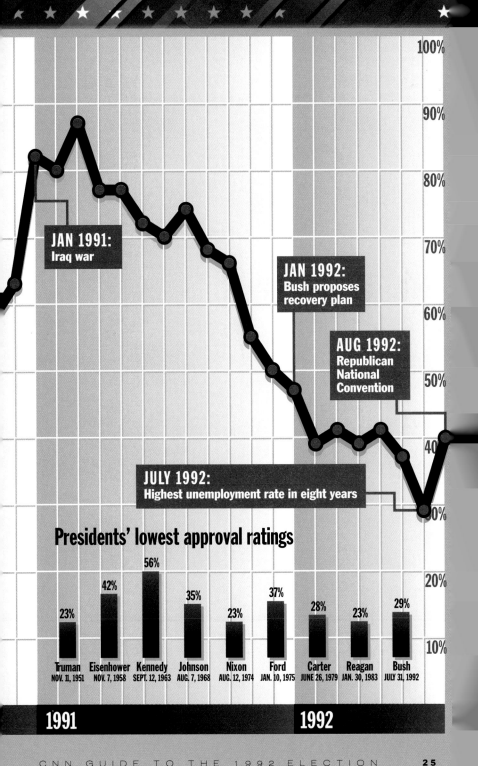

JAN 1991:
Iraq war

JAN 1992:
Bush proposes
recovery plan

AUG 1992:
Republican
National
Convention

JULY 1992:
Highest unemployment rate in eight years

100%
90%
80%
70%
60%
50%
40%
30%
20%
10%

Presidents' lowest approval ratings

Truman NOV. 11, 1951	23%
Eisenhower NOV. 7, 1958	42%
Kennedy SEPT. 12, 1963	56%
Johnson AUG. 7, 1968	35%
Nixon AUG. 12, 1974	23%
Ford JAN. 10, 1975	37%
Carter JUNE 26, 1979	28%
Reagan JAN. 30, 1983	23%
Bush JULY 31, 1992	29%

1991

1992

"A DIFFERENT
KIND OF
FISH"

CHAPTER 1

HARRIS WOFFORD, a 65-year-old, little-known Democrat sounded the basic theme for the 1992 presidential campaign. Wofford defeated Republican Richard Thornburgh in a special Pennsylvania election held in November 1991 to fill a U.S. Senate seat. After starting off nearly 45 points behind Thornburgh, Wofford got 55 percent of the votes, decisively thrashing a consummate politician. Thornburgh, a former two-term governor, had resigned as President Bush's Attorney General to run against Wofford, who had never before run for office.

When the race began, it had little to do with national politics. When it ended, the Democrats had their theme for 1992: change. And the Republicans had a new worry: Bush as a domestic President.

Harris Wofford is sworn into office as U.S. Senator.

Wofford wanted his race to be a national race, one that would convince Democrats that there was a way to win the White House—*challenge the President*. The idea was heresy. The Democratic Party was built around state organizations that focused on House and Senate contests and disdained organizing on the national level. The state-level Democrats did their part by creating Democratic majorities in the House and Senate. Presidential elections came around every four years, and, it seemed, no one knew anymore how to win one.

Now an obscure visionary shook up the system and looked beyond the boundaries of Pennsylvania to find his victory. He portrayed Thornburgh as a major player in an unprincipled system. The former Attorney General's self-professed experience in the "corridors of power," Wofford said, was a good reason for people to vote *against* Thornburgh. Wofford repeatedly quoted a line from campaign aide James Carville: "The idea of Dick Thornburgh coming back to Pennsylvania and saying, 'Send me to the corridors of power because I know Washington,' is like running on a pro-leprosy ticket at the time of Jesus."

Thornburgh, Wofford charged, helped "create the mess in Washington" and was part of the cynical cadre of insiders who had looked the other way while "S&L crooks" cleaned out savings institutions. Wofford ran against Washington, against insiders, against the system. And he won. His victory should have given political leaders of both parties a clear sign that the driving force in the 1992 elections would be a demand for change.

"Harris Wofford road-tested the 1992 Democratic presidential message in Pennsylvania," said Democratic pollster Mark Mellman.

Technically Wofford ran as an incumbent. Democratic Governor Robert Casey appointed Wofford to fill the vacancy created when Republican Senator John Heinz was killed in a plane crash. But Wofford tried to portray himself as an outsider. After only two months in the Senate he repudiated the $23,200 pay raise that the Senate had voted itself. He said he would turn his raise over to a charity for the kin of Gulf War casualties. "There's a national recession out there," he said. "Now is no time for us to be paying ourselves more of our taxpayers' hard-earned dollars."

He also refused to accept the $150,000 that Senators gave themselves for mass-mailing expenses. And he introduced a symbolic bill that would take away from Senators and Representatives the free medical care they get from the government. The ban was to remain in effect until Congress enacted some kind of national health insurance.

"I'm a different kind of fish, who has not been an ordinary politician," Wofford said. "But let me tell you, this is the moment when people around this state don't want an ordinary politician." What elected him in Pennsylvania, Harris Wofford believed, could elect a Democrat as President in 1992.

Republicans were at last vulnerable, he said: "By and large it's hard for them to say that they are the party of change in Washington." But then he added, "That isn't easy for Democrats either, because they have controlled the Congress. Therefore, any individual Democrat who is running better be damned active in proving that he is an agent of change."

Wofford proclaimed change and a disdain for politics while showing himself to be a proper Democrat on populist social issues. He sided with organized labor by denouncing a trade policy that would put "American jobs on a fast track to Mexico." He condemned Thornburgh's call for "a capital gains tax break for the wealthy," an issue favored also by President Bush. Wofford endorsed an extension of unemployment benefits and urged the establishment of a national health-care system. His crowd-pleasing line was, "The constitution says that if you are charged with a crime you have a right to a lawyer. But it's even more fundamental that if you're sick, you should have the right to a doctor."

Faithful as he might be to Democratic tradition, he also saw the need for

Despite George Bush's help, Richard Thornburgh lost the election for U.S. Senator from Pennsylvania.

a transformation of his own party. His message of change for party leaders was, "recognize that we do best and we are strongest when the programs we advance help all the people and are not just targeted programs for the very poor. It's best for the very poor and it's best in getting a consensus that we will uphold action if they're programs that help everybody, such as Social Security and such as national health insurance."

The formula concocted was volatile and complex. It mixed a flagging economy with voter resentment. A recession, which had begun in the summer of 1990, was hurting many parts of the country, including Pennsylvania, where unemployment was inching upwards to 7 percent. Merchants and realtors complained that people were afraid to spend money. Even one of Thornburgh's own aides called Pennsylvania a "sorry assed state."

At the same time, Bush's triumph in the Persian Gulf was being eclipsed by news coming from a homefront under siege. The recession resisted presidential rhetoric about impending recovery. Words could not hide the numbers: higher unemployment rates, more people on welfare, more bankruptcies, more foreclosures, lower industrial production, lower

Wofford, on the hustings, takes his "different kind of fish" to Pennsylvania workers.

Growing unemployment lines defy presidential predictions about the economy.

personal income, and a stagnant real estate market.

The slumping economy alone could not account for Wofford's stunning win. Something was happening deep within the American electoral system. Voters saw a Washington that seemed to have nothing to do with them. While people worried about their jobs and economic future, they read or heard on television stories about congressional check-bouncing and unpaid tabs in the House restaurant.

Amid the economic jitters and anti-politician muttering, Wofford heard what seasoned politicians had not heard—or had ignored. The call from the voters, he said, was "shake Washington up from top to bottom." And the people turning against Washington were people who once had been the mainstay of the Democratic Party, middle-class Americans.

"Republicans win elections by running on populist social issues, like crime, race, and pledging allegiance to the flag," Wofford campaign manager Paul Begala said. "Democrats have to win by concentrating on populist economic issues."

One of the Democrats who immediately grasped the message was Al From, executive director of the Democratic Leadership Council, which had shaped the emerging campaign themes of Arkansas Governor Bill Clinton. Shortly before Wofford's victory, Clinton had announced his candidacy for the Democratic presidential nomination. "Wofford is calling for a fundamental change in the way we do business," From said. "And this is what Democrats need to do to win in 1992."

Wofford warned his party that big government itself was under attack. "If the Democrats take action for national health insurance—not to have a government-run health program but instead to take action that people want—that's part of the answer," he said.

A campaign aide traced Wofford's success to a swift change in voters' worries. Six months before the election, the voters had been concerned about their children and whether they would have a good life as adults. "Now," he said, "they are worried that *they* might not be able to have as good a life as they have now."

The onset of pessimism had indeed been rapid. In February 1991, a nationwide poll showed that 39 percent of voters surveyed believed that "things in the country are off on the wrong track." By the last week in October, 71 percent of the voters agreed with the wrong-track diagnosis. In March, Bush was basking in Gulf War glory and a job performance rating of 89 percent—the highest in the history of the Gallup presidential-approval poll. By late October, as Wofford's victory chances were rising, Bush's approval rating had plummeted to 55 percent. Political observers said the drop coincided with a shift in the mood of the electorate: voters were calling for more attention to domestic issues.

Bush bristled at suggestions that he was better as commander-in-chief than as homefront President. "I am sick and tired of people saying we don't have a domestic agenda," he told Senate Republican leaders shortly after the war ended. "We've got a good one, and with your support we can make it come to pass." But his entreaties to fellow Republicans ignored what was eroding his popularity: the negative effect of his "veto strategy" toward Democratic proposals in Congress, and the blame he was accumulating for the gridlock in government.

Bush may have perceived himself as having a splendid, though muted, domestic policy. But as he himself once admitted to interviewer David Frost, "I'm not good at expressing the concerns of a nation—I'm just not very good at it." And the ability to transmit concern is an essential part of leadership.

Political scientist Paul Quick of the University of Illinois, looking at Bush's achievements in domestic policies in the first two years of office, judged Bush's domestic record as the least effective of any President since the 1920s. Quick granted that Bush was being frustrated by problems with Congress. But, Quick added, Bush's record displayed "his own limitation of style and strategy, his failure to establish a legislative agenda, his willingness to promise least-common-denominator agreements, and, above all, his penchant for rigidity and rhetorical excess, especially on taxes."

Burton Yale Pines, vice president of the conservative Heritage Foundation, put it more bluntly, "George Bush and his White House have only one real goal—to be reelected. Content is relatively unimportant—if not completely unimportant." If reelection was indeed Bush's goal, Wofford's win revealed a massive obstacle between Bush and his goal. The obstacle was change—a change from focusing on international affairs to tending to domestic needs, a change from making speeches to offering specifics, a change from insider to outsider.

Outsider. That was the only believable label an agent of change could wear. Wofford had shown a way to beat the President—shout for change, run against Washington, yell about the economy, seek out the middle class. But his incantation of change would sound hollow if it came from the lips of a candidate of the establishment. An outsider who took Wofford's message to the nation could win the Democratic presidential nomination, perhaps the election. But what Democrat could become a national candidate and still manage to look like an outsider?

Cartoonist's view of George Bush pretending to thrive on domestic issues symbolized by broccoli, which he dislikes.

VOTING

CHAPTER 2

AGAINST

POLITICS

T WAS NOT LONG before Ross Perot played a similar theme on a larger scale—he answered a yearning for a man who talked straight. The President had said to read his lips and then had raised taxes. Bill Clinton had told his Arkansas constituents that he would serve out his term as governor, but was running for President. The voters were looking for what Harris Wofford had claimed to be in Pennsylvania, a "non-politician," a different kind of fish. And in 1992 they were beginning to find them.

Women were running for office in record numbers. Incumbent members of Congress, also in record numbers, were declining to run for reelection. The two phenomena would have direct bearing on the presidential race. And one of the focal points of that change had been the

Dianne Feinstein (left) and Barbara Boxer campaign for California Senate seats.

fight over President Bush's appointment of Clarence Thomas to the Supreme Court.

In September 1991 the all-male, all-white Senate Judiciary Committee split 7-7 on President Bush's nomination of Thomas, a black federal judge, to the Supreme Court. As Thomas's name was about to go to the Senate without a recommendation from the Judiciary Committee, news accounts revealed that Anita Hill, a 35-year-old professor of law at the University of Oklahoma, had given the committee an affidavit accusing the nominee of sexual harassment. Hill, a black woman, said that Thomas had harassed her while she worked for him at the U.S. Department of Education and the Equal Employment Opportunity Commission.

Trying to ignore the uproar over Hill's accusations, the Senate on October 8 decided to go on with the vote on Thomas's nomination. But protests by women's groups—and a march on the Senate by seven Democratic House members—stopped the vote. Senator Joseph Biden, chairman of the Judiciary Committee, scheduled a special hearing on Hill's allegations.

In a riveting televised hearing, Hill testified under oath that Thomas "talked about pornographic materials depicting individuals with large penises or large breasts involved in various sex acts....On several occasions [he] told me graphically of his own sexual prowess." Clarence Thomas

Senator Arlen Specter's questioning of Anita Hill angered many women.

vehemently denied her charges, angrily calling the hearing "a national disgrace" and "a high-tech lynching."

Senators, particularly Republicans Orrin Hatch of Utah and Arlen Specter of Pennsylvania, questioned Hill aggressively. Millions of people, by turns fascinated and disgusted, watched the hearings on television.

Among the viewers were Carol Moseley Braun, a black Democratic politician in Chicago, and Lynn H. Yeakel, a fund-raiser for women's charities in Pennsylvania. Both women were outraged when they saw the way the Senators treated Hill. Independently, each decided to run for the Senate. Many other women, who saw in the men-vs.-a-woman spectacle a classic confrontation over sexual harassment, turned their anger into political action. Months later, one of the most popular buttons at the Democratic National Convention simply said, "I believe Anita."

In the Illinois Democratic primary, Braun beat Senator Alan Dixon, who had never before lost an election. CNN political analyst William Schneider called Dixon "the first casualty of the Clarence Thomas confirmation fight." Exit polls showed that voters who voted for Braun had opposed Thomas's confirmation to the Supreme Court. Dixon was one of the 11 Democratic Senators who voted to put Thomas on the bench.

In the Pennsylvania Democratic primary, Yeakel, who had never before run for office, beat opponents who included Lieutenant Governor Mark Singel. But her real opponent, even in the primary, was Specter. One of her TV commercials showed Specter harshly questioning Hill during the hearings. Yeakel runs in November against Specter, who is seeking his third term. Primary exit polls of Republican voters showed that almost 25 percent of them would vote for her against Specter, while only 17 percent said they would vote against Specter if Singel were the Democratic nominee. That is a vivid example of how the gender gap can affect the Democrats in 1992.

"I believe that the backlash from those hearings is somewhat stronger than anyone has documented," Yeakel said. She saw the hearings as "the turning point for American women in terms of really stepping forward, taking political power, using the vote, using our money to elect the candidates who represent our values and stand for our rights."

Fifty-four percent of U.S. registered voters are women, and in 1988 they had a better voting record than men: 58 percent of women voters cast ballots in 1988, compared to 56 percent of men. In recent presidential elections they have voted more often for the Democratic candidate. But

Lynn Yeakel (left) makes TV appearance. Carol Moseley Braun (right) addresses the DNC.

back in 1960, if only women's votes had counted, Richard M. Nixon, not John F. Kennedy, would have become President. Men, not women, gave Kennedy his narrow victory. Through the rest of the 1960s and 1970s, women generally split their votes evenly between the parties. But in 1980 and 1984, women cast more Democratic ballots than men did.

Thus was born the gender gap, which has caused Republicans so much concern that the party intensified attempts to attract women. The gender gap certainly inspired Ronald Reagan to appoint Sandra Day O'Connor to the Supreme Court. This year, more than ever, Republicans are opening what they call the big tent to women. But polls show that the Republican anti-abortion position is alienating many GOP women.

The Democrats stressed pro-choice on abortion, and had no fight over the platform unlike the Republicans. Their convention in Houston saw a fight between pro-choice women and the platform committee, which was absolutely committed to the party's anti-abortion stand. This has kept the gender gap issue alive. "The Republican Party will never be the majority party unless it changes its position on abortion," said Mary Dent Crisp, founder of the Republican Coalition For Choice. She believes that "two-thirds of Republicans support choice." Says Democratic National Chairman Ron Brown, "We are on the right side of all the women's issues, and the Republicans are on the wrong side....We are going to make an appeal directly for strong support among American women." Democratic strategists believe that women on the ballot—especially as high-visibility

Senate candidates—will boost Clinton's vote. This is particularly true in California, Illinois, and Pennsylvania, where Democratic women candidates won extensive media coverage.

Although Carol Moseley Braun is a veteran Illinois politician, she is running as one of the ultimate "outsiders"—the 1992 tag that every candidate (including Bush) wants. "This is a unique year for the outsider," said Harriet Woods, president of the National Women's Political Caucus. "And women are seen as the outsiders—even when they're inside."

Flowing Through A Loophole

Printed at the top of the invitation to The President's Dinner was GEORGE BUSH. An invitation cost $1,500; for $92,000 a donor got a "photo opportunity" with the President. Bill Clinton, at the start of his campaign, had received more than $2.5 million from lawyers and lobbyists, $1.3 million from finance, real estate, and insurance interests, and $423,000 from the health industry. A study of Clinton's finances, commissioned by CNN, showed that $98,700 came from executives of Goodman Sachs & Co. and their relatives.

"UNIDENTIFIABLE" IACOCCA

Federal law says a person cannot contribute more than $1,000 to a candidate per election and that unions and corporations cannot donate any money to a political campaign. Why didn't the President's guests and Clinton's supporters break the law? The answer is "soft money," contributions that flow through the law's biggest loophole, going to a party or committee, not the candidate.

Recipients of donations over $200 must make their "best efforts" to discover donors' occupations, such as S&L executives. Bush campaign efforts failed to identify the jobs of people who gave a total of $5.2 million, CNN special correspondent Brooks Jackson revealed in a Democracy in America report. Among the unidentifiable donors: a man named Lee Iacocca and a woman named Georgette Mosbacher, wife of the campaign's general chairman, Robert Mosbacher.

Barbara Boxer, one of two women running for the Senate from California, is a five-term Representative, complete with scars—she wrote 143 bouncing checks on the notorious and now-defunct House bank. But she campaigns as an outsider.

The outsider idea is a variation on the basic theme of change. That same theme not only is driving the presidential campaign but also is driving incumbents out of Congress. Not since World War II have so many House and Senate members left Congress voluntarily.

Year of the Woman

"T his is the new world order," Maryland Senator Barbara Mikulski proclaimed during the Democratic National Convention, when she introduced more than 30 Democratic women campaigning for seats in Congress. By the time of the Republican National Convention, the GOP had 42 women, nine of them incumbents, in House races, and one woman running for the Senate.

The National Women's Political Caucus said that more than twice as many women were seeking House seats in 1992, compared to 1990. As primary season was ending, there were 21 women running in the 34 Senate contests of 1992. In California, besides Dianne Feinstein and Barbara Boxer—two Democratic women candidates for the U.S. Senate—35 Republican and Democratic women are seeking congressional seats. In two districts, Republican women are running against Democratic women. There are also four women running for governor as Democrats and numerous candidates for state legislatures from both parties. In Ilinois primaries for Cook County judgships, of the 44 women running, 30 won.

Contributions to women candidates have doubled since 1990, thanks mostly to Emily's List, a women's fund-raising organization that takes its name from an acronym for Early Money Is Like Yeast. In 1990, Emily's List raised $1.5 million for 14 candidates. In 1992, it hopes to raise $5 million for about 38 candidates.

LOUD AND CLEAR REACTION TO SENATE HEARINGS

Cartoonists & Writers Syndicate

In every election year since 1976, at least 90 percent of all congressional incumbents were reelected. But this year at least 71 have announced retirement (or, rarely, a quest for another political office). By the time of the parties' national conventions, 15 members of the House had lost in primaries. The losers included Guy Vander Jagt, a longtime GOP leader and former chairman of the National Republican Congressional Committee, who was beaten by a political newcomer.

In the same Illinois Democratic primary that unseated Alan Dixon,

Carol Moseley Braun, a Democratic politician in Chicago, would be the first black woman in the Senate if she is elected. Lynn H. Yeakel will be running in Pennsylvania. In Kansas, Democrat Gloria O'Dell opposes Senate minority leader Robert J. Dole in what O'Dell's supporters call the "Gloria versus Goliath" race. In Missouri, St. Louis County Councilwoman Geri Rothman-Serot beat 14 competitors, including another woman, in the Democratic primary. Her Republican opponent is incumbent Christopher S. Bond.

Why are there so many women candidates in 1992? Primarily because the men who run both parties have discovered women, a political majority that has often been ignored. Jane Danowitz, executive director of the Women's Campaign Fund, sees 1992 as the moment when women began "capturing the imagination of the electorate." Former Vermont Governor Madeline Kunin points to "women who gained political experience in lower offices. Many thought they would stay there, but then the issues of abortion rights and Clarence Thomas hearings sort of enlarged their stride."

The end of the Cold War brought such domestic issues as education, health care, and urban blight to the fore, and women are often perceived as being more attuned than men to these issues.

"It's no longer the Cold War agenda; it's the domestic agenda," Harriet Woods, president of the National Women's Political Caucus, told CNN correspondent Candy Crowley. "And most voters think that women are really the experts when it comes to caring about people."

"Even if every woman now running for the Senate should make it there," Crowley commented, "the Senate would still be just ten percent female. It would be progress, but the true measure of political equality may not come until the day when so many women run, nobody notices."

several other veterans also went down, including a Congressman who had written 716 bouncing House bank checks. *Chicago Tribune* writer John Margolis said the message was that "nobody's safe." No longer could an incumbent "assume that just because you've been elected ten times—and nobody hates you—that you're going to be elected again."

Most incumbents who marched out of Congress said they left because they could no longer stand the tensions and frustrations of governmental gridlock. They made no mention in their farewell speeches of a little-

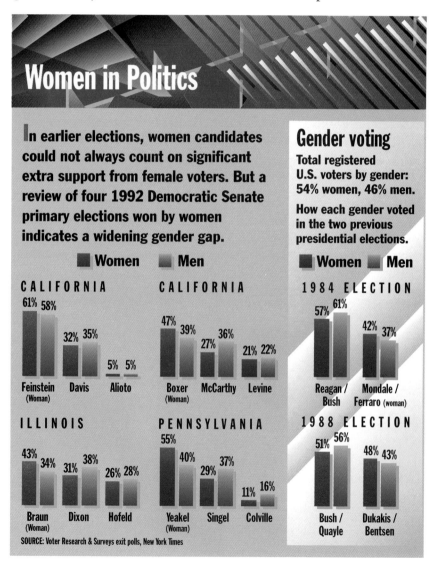

Women in Politics

In earlier elections, women candidates could not always count on significant extra support from female voters. But a review of four 1992 Democratic Senate primary elections won by women indicates a widening gender gap.

■ Women   ■ Men

Gender voting
Total registered U.S. voters by gender: 54% women, 46% men.

How each gender voted in the two previous presidential elections.

■ Women   ■ Men

CALIFORNIA
61% 58%   32% 35%   5% 5%
Feinstein (Woman)   Davis   Alioto

CALIFORNIA
47% 39%   27% 36%   21% 22%
Boxer (Woman)   McCarthy   Levine

1984 ELECTION
57% 61%   42% 37%
Reagan / Bush   Mondale / Ferraro (woman)

ILLINOIS
43% 34%   31% 38%   26% 28%
Braun (Woman)   Dixon   Hofeld

PENNSYLVANIA
55%   40% 29% 37%   11% 16%
Yeakel (Woman)   Singel   Colville

1988 ELECTION
51% 56%   48% 43%
Bush / Quayle   Dukakis / Bentsen

SOURCE: Voter Research & Surveys exit polls, New York Times

publicized fact: House members had paved their exit road in gold. Thanks to a 1979 law they invented and passed, House members can take the leftovers from their campaign contributions. Though the law ends the practice, it sets a deadline of 1992 for eligible members to retain their war-chests. The accumulated amount exceeds $8.6 million. The Senate, where at least seven incumbents announced retirement, does not have such a law.

The financial motivation for leaving was not necessarily paramount, according to House members quoted in the *New York Times*: Representative William S. Broomfield, a Michigan Republican, who is eligible to keep $655,652, said he was leaving because "I have gotten to the point where I have been very, very disgusted with the fact that nothing is going on down there." Representative Brian Donnelly, a Massachusetts Democrat, when he announced his departure, asked, "Why go through the hassle of running from airport to airport and you're still not getting anything done?" He may take $541,521 with him. Representative Lawrence Coughlin, a Pennsylvania Republican, complained about his party being kept out of the legislative process. He can keep $260,846.

A *New York Times* study, backed by data from the Center for Public Integrity, the Federal Election Commission, and the National Taxpayers Union, showed that six Congressmen will get more than $500,000 each. Twenty-seven others can keep sums ranging from $467,600 to $38,742. This war-chest income is in addition to their congressional pensions, which range from $93,510 to $37,084 a year. Twenty-eight of the bounty takers have said they will give the money to political parties or charities. But the *Times* noted that "some retirees who have made such statements in the past have pocketed the money."

As the Congressional exodus was getting under way in March, a CNN/USA *Today* poll asked registered voters, "Do you think most members of the House deserve to be reelected?" Fifty-eight percent said no—an all-time high. When asked if they thought Democrats or Republicans were more to blame for the check bouncing in the House bank, more than three-quarters of them said both parties were equally to blame.

Eighty percent of the voters surveyed said they were dissatisfied and wanted change. Most of them said they did not think that any candidate had any good idea for solving the country's problems. Some voters in Oregon had their ultimate answer for incumbents—and for change. They put up a highway sign that said in big red, white, and blue letters: *Reelect No One.*

TAKING

CHAPTER 3

A CHANCE

ON CHANGE

FOR YEARS THE DEMOCRATS had been blamers and losers. Although they controlled the House and Senate, they wanted the White House, and in four of the last five elections they had lost.

   Then, finally, in 1988, came a candidate the Democrats thought they could beat: George Bush, who they perceived as the perfect WASP and an ill-defined politician who somehow tried to be simultaneously a man of Maine and a Texas cowboy. Many Democrats rushed to battle, plunging into the labyrinth of the Democratic primaries, sounding the trusted party themes. They all came and went: Gary Hart, Joseph Biden, Jesse Jackson, Richard Gephardt, Walter Mondale, Al Gore, Paul Simon, Bruce Babbitt. The one who came and stayed the test was Michael Dukakis, the liberal

Republicans call for change in front of a CNN camera on the convention floor.

governor of Massachusetts, a technocrat. What Democratic leaders most liked about him was that he was not Jesse Jackson.

Although Dukakis began his presidential campaign leading Bush in the polls, Bush soon flattened the Democrat's post-convention bounce, hitting not with issues but with symbols of issues. Bush, who appeared in a flag factory to make his point, questioned Dukakis's patriotism by charging that, as governor, he had been against the saying of the Pledge of Allegiance in schools. The other symbol, questioning Dukakis's record on crime, became one of the most effective TV attack ads in political history: on the screen came the image of prisoners going through a revolving door while a somber voice told how Dukakis as governor gave furloughs to murderers. The ad did not name or picture Willie Horton, a black murderer, who, while on furlough from the Massachusetts prison system, raped a white Maryland woman. But an independent campaign group did show and name Horton.

Bush thoroughly defeated Dukakis, taking 40 states and winning voter groups that ranged from the 18-to-29-year-olds to the 60-plus. Voters with incomes under $12,500 chose Dukakis over Bush two-to-one; Dukakis narrowly won support from voters with incomes of $12,500 to $25,000. A solid majority of voters at all other economic levels voted for Bush.

This time the Democrats had trouble finding a person or phenomenon to blame. They simply seemed to have lost their way. They had also lost the middle class, a traditional source of strength from the New Deal through the Great Society. Shaken by Bush's victory, the Democrats knew that they had to reexamine their policies and goals.

Reagan had created a breed of voter called Reagan Democrats, and Bush kept them. By hammering Democratic candidates on the left, Reagan and Bush showed that Democratic destiny lay toward the center. But the Democrats resisted change in 1988. And, in 1991, as the demoralized Democrats got off to a late, dispirited start, they were groping for a future.

There was no rush to battle in 1991. Bush, commander-in-chief of the Gulf War and the winner of the Cold War, seemed invincible. Al Gore and Dick Gephardt found reasons not to try for the nomination again. So did Jesse Jackson and Senators Sam Nunn and Jay Rockefeller. New York Governor Mario Cuomo, a great hope in 1988, replayed his role in 1991: the non-candidate, waiting.

And so the Democratic field opened to risk-takers willing to run against another unbeatable Republican incumbent. The first to announce was

President and Mrs. Bush tour the allied staging areas after the Gulf War.

former Massachusetts Senator Paul Tsongas, a man whose message was that he would be the best President that Wall Street had ever had.

Tsongas, a collegiate Young Republican and a onetime aide to a Republican Congressman, became a Democrat when the GOP under Reagan moved to the far right. He was a conservative, cautious Democrat. "I am on social issues the most liberal person in this race," he said, "and yet I'm the fiscal disciplinarian." He elaborated his centrist position in an 85-page book, *A Call to Economic Arms*, "a battle plan to strengthen our economic base, better educate our children, and preserve our social fabric."

Tsongas hit at the Reagan-Bush record, blaming them for tripling the national debt, for letting U.S. workers' wages fall, for letting capital from other countries flow into America and buy up U.S. manufacturing plants. Tsongas would reduce capital gains taxes to encourage long-term investment and wring "sacrifices" from voters to restore America's economic and industrial primacy. One of the sacrifices would be an increase in the gasoline tax as part of a complex energy plan to make America less dependent on overseas oil.

Tsongas injected pain and sacrifice—"I'm not Santa Claus"—into the campaign in a curious way, linking his own recovery from cancer with his economic truth-telling. Tsongas retired from the Senate when he was diagnosed as having lymphoma in 1983. He received bone-marrow replacement and recovered. "The one thing I offer to the voter is courage,"

Democratic primary contenders (from left): Paul Tsongas, Tom Harkin...

he said. As a cancer patient, he could not cure himself by avoiding "hard truths"—and neither could a nation struck down by economic ills.

Senator Tom Harkin of Iowa also stepped forward as a candidate and appealed to the traditional populist Democrats. When he made his announcement, he evoked the memory of Franklin D. Roosevelt with an FDR quote from the Great Depression, "We've always known that greed was bad morals. Now we know it's bad economics."

Harkin's economic policy consisted of striking out against "people making money on money" and favoring people who were "making money in agriculture and mining and manufacturing and transportation." He was the first Democratic candidate to weave the end of the Cold War into his speech, asking, "Are you ready for a President who will declare a peace dividend and turn Star Wars into star schools? Are you ready for a President who will give the middle class a break instead of tax breaks for the rich?"

Senator Bob Kerrey of Nebraska, a Vietnam hero, had a gritty, blue-eyed charisma that recalled John F. Kennedy. He vaguely offered "leadership that focuses its attention on posterity rather than popularity." He told how his recovery from wounds led to his intense interest in health care, the issue that would dominate his campaign.

L. Douglas Wilder of Virginia, who in 1989 became the nation's first elected black governor, said he had decided "to rise with the courage of conviction and to serve the country." With Jesse Jackson out of the race, Wilder saw himself as a candidate who could rally the Democrats' most loyal bloc, black voters. He mainly stressed his conservative credentials,

...Bob Kerrey, and Douglas Wilder.

showing his prowess as a budget balancer and administrator.

Former California Governor Edmund G. "Jerry" Brown, Jr., the most experienced of the Democratic candidates, positioned himself as the most outspoken foe of the establishment. Quick to sense the theme of change, Brown assumed the role of outsider. He put aside his long years as a politician, vowing to "do whatever is necessary to bring about real change."

The only white southerner in the race, Governor Bill Clinton of Arkansas offered himself as "proven leadership capable of reinventing government to help solve those real problems real people face." Clinton had been campaigning for years, both as a leader of the nation's governors and as a leader of centrist Democrats. Lunging for the middle-class vote, he proposed to cut their income taxes while providing tax incentives for business investment. When a student asked him if he were calling on the Democratic Party to turn its back on the poor, he replied, "There is no hostility to the poor in my plan. If you're going to help the poor with tax money, somebody's got to earn the money to pay the taxes. The best way to help the poor is to expand the middle class."

In his paean to the middle class, Clinton did not openly acknowledge that he had caught the message of Wofford's victory in Pennsylvania over Thornburgh. But Clinton did sign up the architects of Wofford's campaign, Paul Begala and his partner, James Carville.

The party insiders had another candidate on their minds—New York Governor Mario Cuomo, who was expected to announce his candidacy before the end of the year. Cuomo made his decision 90 minutes before the deadline for filing in the New Hampshire primary. Two chartered aircraft sat on a runway in Albany, ready to whisk Cuomo and reporters to New Hampshire to begin his run for the White House.

The decision was no. "It seems to me," Cuomo said, "I cannot turn my attention to New Hampshire while this threat [New York's fiscal crisis] hangs over the head of the New Yorkers I've sworn to put first." Cuomo's exit further boosted Clinton and Tsongas. In December, Clinton had added to his strength by winning a straw vote at the Florida Democratic convention. He got 54 percent of the vote, compared to 31 for Harkin and 10 for Kerrey.

As the New Hampshire campaign began, the media assigned the candidates to two tiers. In the top tier were Clinton, Kerrey, and Harkin; in the second tier were Wilder, Brown, and Tsongas, whose major advantage in New Hampshire was that he came from neighboring Massachusetts.

While the Democrats lined up for their primaries, the Republicans prepared for the unopposed renomination of George Bush. But two Republicans unexpectedly challenged the President: David Duke and Patrick J. Buchanan. Duke, former Ku Klux Klansman and American Nazi, announced that he spoke for "the grass roots of America." He dismissed his own political roots by saying, "I am not a racist." He then called the

Later, the contest narrowed to Jerry Brown (left) and Bill Clinton.

Democratic Party "the party of Jesse Jackson and Ron Brown," both of whom are black, and said Democrats are "the active agents that are destroying our nation." A Louisiana state representative, he said he would not enter the first of the primaries, in New Hampshire.

In October, Duke had defeated Republican incumbent Governor Buddy Roemer in the Louisiana gubernatorial primary. President Bush and other embarrassed GOP leaders backed Democrat Edwin Edwards in the November runoff election. Edwards won 61 percent of the vote. Undaunted, Duke soon announced his candidacy for the Republican presidential nomination. Republican strategists realized, to their horror, that Duke was not simply going to go away.

Patrick J. Buchanan's announcement as an "America first" candidate came in December. Buchanan was formidable and apparently not of the fringe—he was a conservative with credentials going back to the Nixon Administration. When Buchanan quit CNN's "Crossfire" and announced he was running against Bush, Buchanan supporters shouted, "Revolution!" Picking up that theme, Buchanan tried to show himself to be not a petulant spoiler but a leader who could justly inherit the conservative cause.

"Why am I running?" he asked. "Because we Republicans can no longer say it is all the liberals' fault. It was not some liberal Democrat who declared, 'Read my lips: No new taxes,' then broke his word....What is the White House answer to the recession that was caused by his own breach of faith? It is to deny that we even have a recession. Well, let them come to New Hampshire."

Bush's reneging on his no-new-taxes pledge had given the Democrats an issue they appreciated even more than Buchanan did. Bush's pledge, made in his acceptance speech at the Republican National Convention, had defined his economic agenda. "The Congress will push me to raise taxes, and I'll say no," he told the cheering delegates on August 18, 1988. "And they'll push, and I'll say no. And they'll push again, and I'll say to them, 'Read my lips: No new taxes.'"

The pushing came from the deficit and from the budget, both of which had grown to such size that congressional leaders and Bush knew that they had to make a deal. Bush announced the grim results of the deal on June 26, 1990. He would sign into law a tax agreement that would raise from 28 percent to 31 percent the income tax rate on adjusted gross incomes over $80,000. Gasoline, alcohol, tobacco, and luxury taxes would be raised. The new tax law also wrung more money from payroll taxes and phased out

The theme of the 1992 election quickly became clear.

personal exemptions for taxpayers making more than $100,000 a year.

Bush's popularity had been enhanced by the way he had handled the Persian Gulf crisis and organized the U.S.-led allied forces that defeated Iraq and liberated Kuwait. But while Bush basked in the glow of an international triumph, domestic problems had been stirring in the shadows. In February 1991 the unemployment rate reached 6.5 percent, the highest rate in four years. In March other economic indicators showed that the recession would not die, as the President's Council of Economic Advisers had predicted it would only a month before.

If the economy had not slumped, if unemployment rates had not risen, Bush might have gotten away with breaking his promise. But the recession made the economy a major election-year issue. And voters' thoughts about the economy easily translated into anger over Bush's turnabout on taxes.

Bush, Buchanan said, "is yesterday and we are tomorrow. He is a globalist and we are nationalists....He would put America's wealth and power at the service of some vague new world order. We would put America first."

George Bush, however, still had the advantages of his incumbency, his popularity, and his ability to get headlines and air time without leaving the White House. But Buchanan's relentless attacks jarred Bush from his apathy and his Oval Office. Bush responded to Buchanan's "send a message" line with an echo, "Send a message—to Congress." Bush blamed the Democratic-controlled Congress for New Hampshire's slumping economy and growing unemployment. Accused of not caring about the state's financial plight, he said, "The message: I care." Bush brought Arnold Schwarzenegger along on a New Hampshire trip, and the Terminator sent another message to Pat Buchanan, "Hasta la vista, baby!"

Bush's advisers, caught off guard by Buchanan's surge in popularity, knew that New Hampshire needed more than caring. Unemployment in some towns had hit 10 percent; bankruptcies were up from about 1,000 in 1989 to nearly 3,500 in 1991. And Buchanan had caught the mood. One night he stood on a flatbed truck while a huge searchlight skimmed across an abandoned mill in Manchester. "Where's George?" he asked. As Buchanan and his audience knew, George Bush was in the Far East on what was billed as a trade mission for jobs.

The President tried to show his concern with television ads. In one, a woman said to him, "I have never seen it so bad, where people have to lose their homes…people don't have jobs." Bush cut in to say, "You can give it to me straight because we've known each other for a long time. A lot of you are hurting. I've seen the pain in people's eyes.…This state has gone through hell.…I am determined to turn this state around."

Polls showed Buchanan gaining on Bush. New Hampshire was looking like a place where Bush might also go through hell.

As the Democrats assembled in New Hampshire, the atmosphere began to change. Bush was not invincible. The President had removed the fundamental accusation that Republicans made against Democrats. No longer could Bush say that the Democrats were the tax-raisers and he was

Republican challengers David Duke (left) and Pat Buchanan.

If the economy had not slumped, if unemployment rates had not risen, Bush might have gotten away with breaking his promise. But the recession made the economy a major election-year issue. And voters' thoughts about the economy easily translated into anger over Bush's turnabout on taxes.

Bush, Buchanan said, "is yesterday and we are tomorrow. He is a globalist and we are nationalists….He would put America's wealth and

1992 Democratic Primary Results

State	Date	Turnout	Brown	Clinton	Harkin	Kerrey	Tsongas	Others	Uncom.
New Hampshire	Feb. 18	167,819	8.1%	24.7%	10.2%	11.1%	33.2%	12.7%	—
South Dakota	Feb. 25	59,503	3.9	19.1	25.2	40.2	9.6	2.0	—
Colorado	March 3	239,643	28.8	26.9	2.4	12.3	25.6	1.6	2.2%
Georgia	March 3	454,631	8.1	57.2	2.1	4.8	24.0	—	3.8
Maryland	March 3	567,224	8.2	33.5	5.8	4.8[1]	40.6	0.8	6.4
South Carolina	March 7	116,414	6.0	62.9	6.6[2]	0.5	18.3	2.6	3.1
Florida	March 10	1,123,857	12.4	50.8	1.2	1.1	34.5	—	—
Louisiana	March 10	384,417	6.6	69.5	1.0	0.8	11.1	11.0	—
Massachusetts	March 10	794,093	14.6	10.9	0.5	0.7	66.3	5.5	1.5
Mississippi	March 10	191,357	9.6	73.1	1.3	0.9	8.1	0.8	6.2
Oklahoma	March 10	416,129	16.7	70.5	3.4	3.2	—	11.9	—
Rhode Island	March 10	50,709	18.8	21.2	0.6	0.9	52.9	4.1	1.4
Tennessee	March 10	318.482	8.0	67.3	0.7	0.5	19.4	0.1	3.9
Texas	March 10	1,482,975	8.0	65.6	1.3	1.4	19.2	4.5	—
Illinois	March 17	1,504,130	14.6	51.6	2.0	0.7	25.8	0.7	4.5
Michigan	March 17	585,972	25.8	50.7	1.1	0.0	16.6[3]	0.5	4.8
Connecticut	March 24	173,119	37.2	35.6	1.1	0.7	19.5	2.7	3.1
Puerto Rico	April 5	63,398	1.6	95.6	0.0	1.3	0.1	1.0	0.3
Kansas	April 7	160,251	13.0	51.3	0.6	1.4	15.2	4.7	13.8
Minnesota	April 7	204,170	30.6	31.1	2.0	0.6	21.3	8.8[4]	5.6
New York	April 7	1,007,726	26.2	40.9	1.1	1.1	28.6	2.0	—
Wisconsin	April 7	772.596	34.5	37.2	0.7	0.4	21.8	3.4	2.0
Pennsylvania	April 28	1,265,495	25.7	56.5	1.7	1.6	12.8	1.7	—
Dist. of Columbia	May 5	61,904	7.2	73.8	—	—	10.4	—	8.5
Indiana	May 5	476,850	21.5	63.3	—	3.0	12.2	—	—

power at the service of some vague new world order. We would put America first."

George Bush, however, still had the advantages of his incumbency, his popularity, and his ability to get headlines and air time without leaving the White House. But Buchanan's relentless attacks jarred Bush from his apathy and his Oval Office. Bush responded to Buchanan's "send a

State	Date	Turnout	Brown	Clinton	Harkin	Kerrey	Tsongas	Others	Uncom.
North Carolina	May 5	691,875	10.4	64.1	0.9	0.9	8.3	—	15.4
Nebraska	May 12	150,587	21.0	45.5	2.8	—	7.1	7.1	16.4
West Virginia	May 12	306,866	11.9	74.2	0.9	1.0	6.9	5.0	—
Oregon	May 19	347,698	31.4	45.3	—	—	10.5	12.7	—
Washington[*]	May 19	147,981	23.1	42.0	1.3	1.0	12.8	19.8[4]	—
Arkansas	May 26	502,617	11.0	68.0	—	—	—	2.9	18.0
Idaho	May 26	55,124	16.7	49.0	—	—	—	5.2	29.1
Kentucky	May 26	369,438	8.3	56.0	1.9	0.9	4.9	—	28.0
Alabama	June 2	450,899	6.8	68.2	—	—	—	4.8	20.2
California	June 2	2,752,029	40.2	47.5	—	1.2	7.4	3.8	—
Montana	June 2	116,899	18.5	46.9	—	—	10.8	—	23.9
New Jersey	June 2	399,913	19.5	59.2	—	—	11.1	2.9	7.3
New Mexico	June 2	180,770	16.9	52.8	1.9	—	6.3	2.8	19.4
Ohio	June 2	1,032,851	19.0	61.2	2.4	2.2	10.6	4.6	—
North Dakota[*]	June 9	31,562	—	12.6[5]	—	—	—	87.4[4]	—

[1] Kerrey withdrew from the race March 5.

[2] Harkin withdrew from the race March 9.

[3] Tsongas withdrew from the race March 19.

[4] Perot write-in votes totaled 2.1 percent of the Democratic primary vote in Minnesota, 19.1 percent in Washington, and 28.4 percent in North Dakota (which was the winning total).

[5] Clinton's vote in North Dakota came on write-ins.

[*] Indicates a non-binding "beauty contest" primary.

— indicates that the candidate or the uncommitted line was not listed on the ballot.

NOTE: Results are based on official returns except for California, Montana, New Jersey, New Mexico, North Dakota, Ohio, Oregon, and Puerto Rico, where results are nearly complete but unofficial. Percentages may not add to 100 due to rounding.

CLINTON'S

RISE AND

FALL

CHAPTER 4

I N THE NEW HAMPSHIRE primary the man to bet on was Arkansas
Governor Bill Clinton. He had raised considerable money and put together
a nationwide organization. He also had won the support of Democrats who
had been trying to pull the party away from the left and toward the center.
Their vehicle was the Democratic Leadership Council, which emerged in
the spring of 1985 following former Vice President Walter F. Mondale's
cataclysmic 49-state loss to President Ronald Reagan.

There had been speculation that Senator Sam Nunn of Georgia or
Senator Al Gore of Tennessee would be the council-launched candidate in
1992. They, along with Clinton, were among the founders of the council.
When Nunn and Gore stayed out of the race during the short Bush-on-top

Bill Clinton smiles confidently on the eve of the New Hampshire primary.

period of 1991, Clinton looked like a possible DLC aspirant. As an ambitious southern politician, he had the credentials to present himself as a moderate nominee for President or Vice President. But he could not make his move in 1992 because of his full-term pledge to Arkansas voters. Or so it seemed.

In 1990, when Clinton had run for reelection to his fifth term as governor, Arkansas voters wanted a pledge, and they got it. He promised that if they reelected him he would not run for President in 1992 and would serve out his four-year term. They did reelect him, but, as he began his fifth term, he became chairman of the DLC, and it soon became apparent that his ambition was taking him beyond Little Rock.

In May 1991 Clinton went to Cleveland for the DLC's annual meeting, a forum that would give him national exposure to the media and to influential Democrats from all over the country. "Too many of the people who used to vote for us, the very burdened middle class we're talking about," Clinton told the gathering, "have not trusted us in national elections to defend our national interests abroad, to put their values in our social policy at home, or to take their tax money and spend it with discipline." His "New Covenant" was actually a blueprint for the building of a new Democratic Party: economic opportunity for business *and* the poor, aid to the urban poor *and* the middle class, a welfare system of government checks *and* work.

Three months after the Cleveland meeting, Clinton made what became known as "The Secret Trip," an unpublicized journey around Arkansas to learn what voters would say if their governor made a bid for the presidency. He had successfully pushed through the legislature a 0.5 percent increase in the state corporate income tax to pay for improvements in Arkansas colleges and vocational schools. He pointed to accomplishments like that and told voters that, as a governor, he had done all he could for Arkansas. In order to accomplish any more, he had to become President. Clinton ended the trip convinced that most of the people he talked to would accept his breaking of the pledge.

So Clinton announced his candidacy in October and followed with a speech in Chicago to the Association of Democratic State Chairs. The party leaders looked him over and discovered that, while he was a DLCer with the conservatism those initials implied, he could still sound like a genuine Democrat. Accused of being a "warmed-over Republican," Clinton said, "I am a Democrat by heritage, instinct, and conviction. When my grandfather died, he thought he was going to Franklin Roosevelt."

Despite his pledge to serve out his four-year term as Arkansas governor, Clinton announced his candidacy for President in October 1991.

Clinton did not just bash Bush. He had proposals, well packaged and well presented. He did not just have ideas about the future. He could lay out an economic plan. He promised to work for a 10 percent tax cut that would benefit families in the 15 and 28 percent tax brackets and for a tax hike on incomes over $200,000.

To DLC theorists, Clinton looked like the most appealing candidate. They pushed his cause, telling Democratic leaders and media heavyweights what they saw as indisputable reality: the Democrats, after losing five out of the last six presidential elections, had the best chance to win by nominating a centrist from the South. And that centrist looked like Clinton.

Between his well-received appearance in Chicago and the beginning of 1992, Clinton raised about $3.3 million—almost as much as the total funds of all his rivals—and entered the election year as a well-financed front runner. Much of the money came from contributors who had expected to write checks for Mario Cuomo.

As the campaigners and their media trackers set up their quadrennial bivouacs in New Hampshire in the new year, the polls showed that Clinton was leading the Democratic pack. He was a dynamic, tireless campaigner. Crowds swarmed around him. Harkin, Kerrey, Brown, and Tsongas gamely kept on slogging around the state. (Wilder, who had barely campaigned, disappeared as quietly as he had appeared.) Clinton and his advisers saw a win in this first primary as the kickoff to a string of wins. Only Tsongas, the former Massachusetts Senator, seemed likely to come close. Before Clinton began campaigning, Tsongas had been expected to beat Clinton or any other southerner in New Hampshire. Now Clinton, the man from Hope, Arkansas, was on top.

On Sunday, January 19, the Democratic candidates gathered in Manchester for a televised debate. The moderator, National Public Radio's Cokie Roberts, asked Clinton whether he believed that he would be hurt by rumors that he had had affairs with several women. "I think the American people are sick and tired of that kind of negative politics," Clinton replied. "They want somebody who can lead."

Television and newspaper coverage of the debate passed over the womanizing query and focused on Clinton's popular proposal, a tax cut for the middle class. This was the major issue over which Clinton and Tsongas clashed.

"I'm not for the middle-class tax cut because it doesn't work," Tsongas declared steadfastly. "…What I've tried to do is to look at economic truth." Tsongas's persistent tough talk about economics and sacrifice seemed to be denying him the lead in the polls. What was driving Clinton ahead was his energy and confidence. He was beginning to look like a winner, and that helped make him a winner.

The question about marital fidelity had been expected. Clinton's wife, Hillary, at first had opposed his run for the presidency. Among her reasons was concern that there would be national replay of the gossip that had slithered through the 1990 gubernatorial campaign. The source of the gossip was Larry Nichols, a state employee who had been fired. Nichols had filed a civil suit charging that Clinton had carried on affairs with five women. The Arkansas media ignored the claims after off-the-record meetings between Clinton and key reporters and editors. Clinton had denied Nichols's charges while admitting that he and Hillary had had marital problems.

Hillary Clinton soon came around to endorsing her husband's decision to run. "I told Bill," she later recalled, "that if the government was doing what it should—improving our schools, health care, eradicating poverty—then he didn't need to be President. But since the government wasn't doing those things, it was worth the negative stories he might face to run for President."

Months before the primary season, Clinton tried to forestall the infidelity issue by making a preemptive move at a meeting with Washington reporters. The session took place at a gathering that was a Washington institution, the eat-and-ask breakfast served up regularly by *Christian Science Monitor* correspondent Godfrey Sperling. Clinton and his wife attended together.

In response to expected questions about the state of their marriage, Clinton said, "We love each other very much. Like nearly everybody who's been together 20 years, our relationship has not been perfect or free of difficulties but we feel good about where we are." He later added, "We intend to be together 30 or 40 years from now, whether I run for President or not, and I think that ought to be enough."

Cokie Roberts's question had been inspired by stories that had appeared

Hillary Clinton's strong support of her husband and her public statements prompted "Vote for Hillary" bumper stickers.

A supermarket tabloid, *The Star*, exploited Clinton's alleged liaison with Gennifer Flowers, a state employee.

on January 17 in *The Boston Herald* and two New York City tabloids, *The New York Post* and *The Daily News*. The stories had reported that a supermarket tabloid, *The Star*, was about to hit the checkout lines with a feature resurrecting the Nichols civil suit. When *The Star* did come out, Clinton's aides successfully played down the article, and the major national media essentially ignored it.

The Star, however, had more to tell. The following week it named one of the women making the allegations, Gennifer Flowers, a receptionist at the Arkansas unemployment office appeals board and a former nightclub singer. The story said that she had had an affair with Clinton from 1977 to 1989. A year before, in 1990, Flowers had threatened to sue a Little Rock radio station for having "wrongfully and untruthfully" alleged such an affair. But now she was backing up her story with alleged tape recordings of telephone calls.

Clinton's staff, after negotiating with ABC for an appearance on "Nightline" and with CNN to put him on "Newsmaker Saturday," chose instead an interview of both Clintons on the CBS News show "60 Minutes."

The interview was taped on Sunday afternoon in a Boston hotel room and broadcast that night after the Super Bowl game. An audience estimated at more than 34 million saw Bill and Hillary Clinton sitting together, almost clinging to each other, while they answered questions from CBS correspondent Steve Kroft.

"I have acknowledged wrongdoing," Clinton said. "I have acknowledged causing pain in my marriage."

"Who is Gennifer Flowers?" Kroft asked. "You know her?"

"Oh, yes," Clinton replied, saying that their relationship was "very limited, but until this, you know, friendly but limited." Hillary Clinton said she also knew Flowers.

"Bill talked to this woman every time she called, distraught, saying her life was going to be ruined," Hillary Clinton recalled. "...He'd get off the phone and tell me that she said sort of wacky things, which we thought were attributable to the fact that she was terrified."

When asked directly about Flowers's allegation, Clinton said, "That allegation is false....I said that before. And so has she."

Kroft returned to Clinton's reference to marital troubles, "What do you mean by that? What does that mean? Is that some kind of—help us break the code. I mean, does it mean that you were separated? Does that mean that you had communication problems? Does that mean you contemplated divorce? Does it mean adultery?"

Clinton replied, "I think the American people, at least the people that have been married for a long time, know what it means and know the whole range of things it can mean."

Kroft persisted, "You've been saying all week that you've got to put this issue behind you. Are you prepared tonight to say that you've never had an extramarital affair?"

Clinton said he believed that married couples should not discuss such matters "with anyone but themselves....I have said things to you tonight and to the American people from the beginning that no American politician ever has....I think most Americans who are watching this tonight, they'll know what we're saying; they'll get it....And I think what the press has to decide is: are we going to engage in a game of 'gotcha'?"

When Kroft remarked that it appeared that "you've seemed to reach some sort of understanding and arrangement," both Clintons angrily reacted.

"Wait a minute, wait a minute, wait a minute," Bill Clinton said. "You're looking at two people who love each other. This is not an arrangement or an understanding. This is a marriage. That's a very different thing."

Hillary Clinton, who had not been heard or seen by many Americans until that night, cut in to say, "You know, I'm not sitting here—some little woman standing by my man like Tammy Wynette. I'm sitting here because I love him, and I respect him, and I honor what he's been through and what we've been through together. And, you know, if that's not enough for people, then, heck, don't vote for him."

When the taping ended, Bill Clinton returned to New Hampshire for a few hours, then flew to Little Rock. He and Hillary Clinton, who had returned earlier, watched the interview at their home. With them was their 12-year-old daughter Chelsea. "It was pretty painful," Clinton said later. When it was over, he turned to Chelsea and asked, "What do you think?" She replied, "I'm glad you're my parents."

In a televised press conference, Gennifer Flowers replied to the Clintons' "60 Minutes" interview. "Yes, I was Bill Clinton's lover for 12 years," she said. "And for the past two years I have lied to the press about our relationship to protect him. The truth is I loved him. Now he tells me to deny it. Well, I'm sick of all the deceits and I'm sick of all the lies. Last night I sat and watched Bill on '60 Minutes.' I felt disgusted, and I saw a side of Bill I have never seen before. He is absolutely lying....The man on '60 Minutes' was not the man I fell in love with." Two days after the press

In New Hampshire, Clinton and his daughter, Chelsea, watch from the wings while Hillary addresses the crowd.

Gennifer Flowers responds to reporters' questions at news conference where tapes of telephone conversations are aired.

conference, Flowers was fired from her state job for unexcused absences.

The Star, which had paid an undisclosed sum for Flowers's accusations, released alleged transcripts of Clinton-Flowers phone calls saying that the calls were taped between September and December 1991. Clinton questioned the authenticity of the tapes.

CNN, which aired some of the tapes, had a forensic expert check them. He said that there had been some light editing. Clinton's panicky aides seized on this, trying to cast doubt on the conversations. But Clinton himself indirectly verified at least one exchange. The male on a tape says, "Cuomo's at 87 percent name recognition, and I have 54 percent." The woman says, "Well, I don't particularly care for Cuomo's uh, demeanor...he seems like he could get real mean [laughs]...I wouldn't be surprised if he didn't have some Mafioso major connections." "Well he acts like one," the man says, laughing. Cuomo later revealed that Clinton apologized for the remark, thereby inadvertently admitting the voice was his. In the following tape segment, *The Star* identified the voices as those of Clinton and Flowers.

Clinton: I'll tell you what. It would be extremely valuable if they ever do run anybody by me, you know. If they ever get anybody to do this, just to have, like I told you before when I called you, is to have an on-file affidavit explaining that, you know, you were approached by a Republican and asked to do that.

Flowers: Mm hmm. Well…

Clinton: [garbled] …the more I think about it, you should call him back. …[garbled]…just don't know.

Flowers: Well, I think that…Well, are you going to run? [laughs] Can you tell me that?

Clinton: I want to. I wonder if I'm going to be blown out of the water with this. I don't see how they can [garbled word] so far.

Flowers: I don't think they can.…

Clinton: If they don't, if they don't have pictures.…

Flowers: Mh hmm.

Clinton: …and no one says anything then they don't have anything and arguably if someone says something, they don't have much.

Flowers: If they could blow you out of the water, they would have already blown you. I really believe that because I believe that there are various ones that have been trying hard lately. See, like that "Inside Edition" [television show]. Uh, there've probably been other sources too. [Pause] So…I don't think so. I honestly don't. That's my gut feeling.…"

The "60 Minutes" appearance seemed to have put Clinton back on track in New Hampshire. His advisers were congratulating themselves on their damage control efforts when *The Wall Street Journal* resurrected a draft-dodger accusation that had first surfaced during Clinton's successful campaign for governor in 1978. The story was that he had disavowed a commitment to enter the advanced Reserve Officers' Training Corps at the University of Arkansas in 1969. The ROTC obligation was made in exchange for a deferment from the draft. So, the accusation went, by getting and then backing out of the commitment, Clinton got a reprieve from the Vietnam War.

Clinton repeated what he had said in the 1978 Arkansas campaign—that the ROTC commitment was canceled and the deferment never came. Although the *Journal* story added a few details, it was essentially a charge that Clinton had fielded before. The campaign staff, though jittery, felt the worst had past. On February 7, Clinton decided to fly to Little Rock for the

Clinton meets his hero, John F. Kennedy, at a high school leadership conference in Washington, D.C. Even then, Clinton was planning a political career.

weekend. Meanwhile, polls showed that Clinton had dropped 17 points. A campaign aide had a word for it: "meltdown."

On Monday, when Clinton and his troubled aides returned to New Hampshire, a reporter for ABC handed Clinton a copy of a letter he had written in 1969 to Col. Eugene Holmes of the Arkansas ROTC, thanking the officer for "saving" him from the draft. Clinton wrote the letter while he was on a Rhodes scholarship at Oxford. In the letter he admitted a struggle of conscience between going into the military and continuing his studies. He said he knew that his avoiding of the draft would becloud his "political viability." Even while he was in college—some say even while he was in high school—he had planned to become a politician.

Clinton blasted the "Republican attack machine"—an unsubstantiated charge—and fumed over the way the campaign had "descended into a bizarre series of diversions" that had "nothing to do with the hopes and dreams, the crises and fears of the people of New Hampshire."

He set off on an exhausting five-day trip, vowing to New Hampshire voters, "I'll never forget who gave me a second chance." And he said he would never forget the signs of despair and economic gloom he had seen in the state. "I'll fight like hell," he said. "I'll fight until the last dog dies."

THE

CHAPTER 5

COMEBACK

AS THE SHOWDOWN NEARED in New Hampshire, the theme of the primary election was no longer the state's idle mills or the high cost of health care. Suddenly, the theme was character. *The Boston Herald*, endorsing Tsongas over Clinton, proclaimed the change. The newspaper lauded Tsongas's "strength of character" and said, "At a time when voters are weary of candidates with feet of clay, Paul Tsongas is a man whose integrity is unquestioned."

In the New Hampshire campaign's final days, Clinton was still fighting off accusations of infidelity and draft dodging. "For too much of the last couple of weeks," he complained, "this election has been about me." Responding to "character" as an issue, he said, "The real character issue and the real patriotism issue in this election is, who has a vision for the country, a plan for the future and the ability to get it done. The people whose character and patriotism is really an issue in this election are those who would divert the attention of the people, who destroy the reputations of their opponents and divide the country we love."

In 1988, character had been a code word for Gary Hart's adultery. In 1992, character encompassed a more fundamental voter concern: trust of politicians. Character meant honor, honesty, integrity, not merely in

Nomination almost assured, Bill Clinton "sends a message" on the Arsenio Hall show.

personal conduct but, more importantly, in public office. Candidates were facing an electorate that had been lied to about Vietnam, about Watergate, about Iran-Contra, about the savings and loan scandal—and who now fumed over a Congress bouncing checks and a Senate slipping itself a raise in the middle of the night. "Politician is a dirty word," a prospective voter said in a CNN special on the New Hampshire primary. "People are fed up."

Tsongas, riding his "I'm-no-Santa-Claus" theme, ignored Clinton's character and concentrated on the economy. He argued that the Democratic Party had to abandon its liberal ways and focus on developing an economic policy. "I decided to run to rescue the nation's economy," he said in a televised debate. "You cannot do that with giveaways and tax breaks....My job is to rescue this country so people can have a job . . . so they can provide for their families."

Harkin stayed with his "new New Deal," affirming his faith in liberalism and its appeal to people—"Let's put them to work, start educating our kids, and let's have a national health insurance program. That's bottom-up, percolate-up economics, not trickle-down economics."

Brown, continuing to play his role as guerrilla candidate against the party regulars, ignored issues to hammer at voter bitterness toward the system, "I think people are frustrated. They're angry. They look out at America and they know we're strong. We're the richest country in the world and yet what's happening? Our automobile industry is declining. Our ports are not competing. Our shipping industry is a shadow of what it once was. Our cities are deteriorating....We need real reform."

A major emerging issue was health care, an issue that Kerrey acted as if he owned. Responding to Bush's plan, unveiled in the President's State of the Union message, Kerrey called Bush "the witch doctor of American health care." Clinton dismissed the Bush plan as "another set of Band-Aids, designed to make it look like they're doing something when they're not." Harkin labeled it "wasteful and inefficient." Tsongas said the plan "has no credence with any of the health-care professionals." When the smoke cleared from this fusillade, voters still saw the issue, though not the details and the costs that set off one plan from the other.

By far the candidate with the most money, Clinton bought television time for a call-in show, buzzed around the state in a chartered plane, and passed out more than 20,000 videotapes showing Clinton, the man and the candidate. The tapes were handed out free to VCR owners by house-to-house volunteer distributors and added a new device to a high-tech election campaign that was whirling away from traditional vote-getting tactics. Clinton officials later claimed that almost 50 percent of the undecided voters who saw the video decided to vote for Clinton.

The actual Democratic results, in percentages, were: Tsongas 33, Clinton 25, Kerrey 11, Harkin 10, Brown 8. Non-candidate Cuomo (who had not disavowed a write-in effort) got 4 percent of the vote, and others, including the veteran consumer advocate Ralph Nader, got 9.

On the GOP side, Bush won 53 percent of the New Hampshire vote, to Buchanan's 37 percent; 10 percent was scattered among others. Bush had won, but he had also not won. A national survey by CNN/USA *Today* showed that his job-approval rating had fallen to an all-time low of 39 percent. And Buchanan seemed to be showing a post–New Hampshire bounce. An overwhelming number of Republicans believed Bush would get the presidential nomination. Yet they wanted Buchanan to keep on challenging Bush; by a two-to-one margin, Republicans polled said Buchanan should stay in the campaign.

"After New Hampshire," said CNN political commentator David S. Broder, "no one can doubt that George Bush must recast his presidency—

"I'm-not-Santa-Claus" Tsongas chats up New Hampshire voters before winning the primary with 33 percent of the votes.

not just his campaign, but his government—if he is going to win a second term. And after New Hampshire, it is equally certain that the Democratic Party is finally ready for change."

The change for the Democrats, at least temporarily, looked like Tsongas. And that set off concerned reactions among the party's leadership. In Washington, quiet, off-the-record soundings were made to Senator Lloyd Bentsen of Texas, who had run with Dukakis in 1988, and to those who had counted themselves out—Gore, Gephardt, and Jay Rockefeller. And, despite his I-shall-not-run stance, there was still Cuomo, the favorite of Democrats surveyed in the CNN/USA *Today* poll.

Acting as if he had come in first in New Hampshire, Clinton paid no attention to rumors of a hunt for new candidates. He told reporters that he felt "liberated" by the results in New Hampshire. On election day, anticipating a Tsongas victory, Clinton speech writers found the line their candidate would use to launch himself into the rest of the primaries. Responding to his second-place finish as if it were a triumph, he told an election-night rally, "New Hampshire has made me the comeback kid."

Though Tsongas profited from Clinton's problems, Clinton still dominated the race. His priority now became to eliminate his weak and impoverished rivals, beginning with Tsongas, who was vulnerable in several ways. Clinton advisers felt that by trying to take the Democratic Party to the center, Tsongas had moved too far to the right. Bush, in fact, said that Tsongas's economic agenda "sounded like" a Republican idea. the Clinton camp also thought that Tsongas did not have that mysterious quality known as electability. Democratic leaders privately agreed with the sentiment, if not the words, of acid-tongued political writer and consultant Kevin Phillips, who said, the Democrats "can't afford to nominate a recovered cancer patient with a speech impediment."

Clinton threw away the script he had used in New Hampshire. Instead of talking about a nation of opportunity and responsibility, he attacked the policies of the Democrats running against him, especially Tsongas.

While Clinton's economic programs brought him early attention, they had not been fully developed. In the first primaries he called for both a middle-class tax cut and a tax credit for families with children. Later, he wavered. He had no overarching economic concept, except for his vague hope to "reinvent government." Against Tsongas, Clinton's blurry economic policy hurt him.

Conceding Maine and Maryland to Tsongas, Clinton worked on a

Combining door-to-door campaigning in New Hampshire with an unusual way to use technology, Clinton hands out some of the 20,000 videotapes promoting himself.

southern strategy. One of the creations of the Dixie-dominated Democratic Leadership Council was Super Tuesday, the one-day clustering of primaries, most of them in the South. The idea was to force candidates to give heed to the region and its conservative philosophy. Clinton headed for Georgia, whose March 3 primary was the prelude to the March 10 Super Tuesday balloting.

Clinton owned Georgia. Tsongas had neither the resources nor the southern connections to challenge him. Kerrey, suffering from the same afflictions, staged an Atlanta press conference and left the state. The Georgia contest between Clinton and Tsongas turned into a nasty fight.

One day, Clinton, not knowing he was speaking into an open mike, raged about Jesse Jackson. Clinton had just heard what turned out to be a false report that Jackson was going to support Harkin. "It's a dirty, double-crossing, back-stabbing thing to do," Clinton said. Tsongas quickly put out a radio spot aimed at Georgia's black vote. A black announcer repeated Clinton's words and said that he had "accused Reverend Jackson" before "he got all the facts." Clinton called the Tsongas commercial "sort of a low-class thing to do." During a debate, he said to Tsongas, "no one can argue with you, Paul; you're always perfect." Tsongas shot back, "I may not be perfect. But I'm honest."

Meanwhile, Republican Buchanan stumped Georgia for the conservative white vote, emphasizing his opposition to what he called racial entitlements. "The South ought to come out of the penalty box," he said. One of his TV commercials attacked Bush for signing the 1991 Civil Rights Act.

Buchanan also continued to attack the President for reneging on his "no new taxes" pledge. Bush soon responded by saying of the tax-raising budget deal, "I thought this one compromise—and it was a compromise—would result in no more tax increases, and so I'm disappointed. And, given all of that, yes, a mistake." Bush would be plagued by this admission. It meant that what he had touted as a keystone of his economic policy was, in fact, a miscalculation.

Yet Bush easily swept the March 3 primaries, taking Georgia, Maryland, and Colorado. Buchanan shouted at supporters, "We can win this nomination!" No one believed him, but Bush's advisers knew that in the general election he would have to win back voters who had gone to the right for Buchanan.

Clinton won Georgia, taking 57 percent of the vote to 24 for Tsongas. Brown and Kerrey came in with low numbers. Harkin got fewer votes than "uncommitted." Tsongas, who had won a Maine caucus, proved he could win outside New England with a victory in Maryland. But, earlier, in South Dakota, he had come in fourth—behind Kerrey, Harkin, and Clinton. So the Maryland win was not solid proof of his vote-getting power beyond New England.

CNN's Bill Schneider, looking at the relationship of voters and income, saw Tsongas getting only 12 percent of the poor's vote, 26 percent of the middle-class vote, and 41 percent from the wealthy. "The Clinton vote, in

Though Buchanan was portrayed by some commentators as a nuisance, he articulated the concerns of the Republican right.

three categories of income," Schneider said, "shrinks as income goes up. Clinton is still very much the populist."

Two clouds, however, hung over the Georgia victory. Turnout was low—as it would be in most Democratic primaries—and polls showed that people who voted for Clinton nevertheless distrusted him. So, although his draft record and Gennifer Flowers had not cost him a numerical victory, they had cost him trust. As a centrist, he could win the Democratic nomination. But he had yet to show that "Slick Willy," as some called him back in Arkansas, could win the presidency.

At stake on Super Tuesday, March 10, were 783 Democratic delegates, well more than one-third of the 2,145 needed for the nomination. By then, Kerrey had dropped out, and Harkin shortly followed. Brown, with a caucus win in Nevada, hung in the race. Clinton went into Super Tuesday after beating Tsongas in South Carolina. Tsongas's last chance to stay in the race was to make a good showing.

The geographic spread was vast—Florida, Louisiana, Mississippi, Missouri, Tennessee, Texas, Oklahoma, Massachusetts, and Rhode Island. Clinton pulled off a Super Tuesday triple play: he staged a baseball-and-baseball-cap photo opportunity at the Houston Astros training camp in Orlando, Florida, when the Astros were playing the Boston Red Sox. The maneuver gave him media coverage in three widely separated Super Tuesday states. On election night, he hit a home run.

"It is only tonight," a grinning Bill Clinton told his followers after the tabulations, "that I fully understand why they call this Super Tuesday." He won Texas, Florida, Oklahoma, Mississippi, Louisiana, Tennessee, and Missouri, getting about 2.2 million votes—some 1 million more than Michael Dukakis got in the South in Super Tuesday in 1988.

Exit polls, according to CNN's Schneider, showed that Clinton "created that biracial populist coalition that Democrats in the South dream about—the poor whites, blacks, and Hispanics." Eight out of 10 black voters chose Clinton, as did about 6 out of 10 Mexican-Americans in Texas, and more than two-thirds of white voters with incomes under $15,000. He also got two-thirds of the union vote.

Tsongas, who took his own state of Massachusetts, along with Rhode Island and Delaware, had this to say about the results of the multistate primary day: "Super Tuesday was meant to eliminate somebody like me. Well, I'm still there." He was right about the architecture of Super Tuesday.

And, though Tsongas was still there, he would have to fight to remain.

President Bush swept all the states with Republican primaries, reaping some 70 percent of the vote; Duke got only 7 percent and Buchanan the remainder. Ex-Klansman Duke would drop out in April. Buchanan managed to find a nugget in the ballot rockfall that hit him, "We have torn away one-third of the Republican Party from the national establishment—for good." While the Republicans were voting overwhelmingly for their President, Bush's approval rating was less than half of what it had been a year ago.

As activity moved from the South to the Midwest, Clinton's dealing with labor unions came under attack. As Gore in 1988 alerted the Republicans to Willie Horton, Tsongas and Brown raised issues that Republicans could exploit in 1992. In Michigan, Brown, wearing a United Auto Workers jacket, said Clinton's labor record as governor "reflects a plantation mentality." Michigan had about 700,000 union members and Illinois about 1.3 million. All three Democratic candidates went after what had always been called the union vote. But did it still exist?

"I don't think the unions are as strong as they used to be," a Chicago union worker said on CNN. "And I think people are just going to vote the way they feel they want to." Another union member admitted having voted for Bush in 1988, "and he might be the front-runner in my mind." Leaders of several unions that had backed Harkin met and declined to endorse

Hillary Clinton makes "cookies" comment about her role as wife and mother.

anyone. But in Michigan leaders of the Teamsters, electrical workers, and metal trade unions urged members to vote for Brown.

Brown and Clinton, virtually ignoring Tsongas, turned the Midwest primaries into a duel beginning with a Democratic debate in Chicago. Brown accused Clinton of using his power as governor to send business to Hillary Clinton's law firm in Little Rock. Clinton angrily denied the charge.

Then his wife threw in her response, with a line that would haunt Clinton's campaign, "You know, I suppose I could have stayed home and baked cookies and had teas." Hillary Clinton went on to say that she had decided "to fulfill my profession, which I entered before my husband was in public life. And I've tried very, very hard to be as careful as possible."

Clinton took Illinois and Michigan, proving, said Schneider, that he "could put together a populist coalition of blacks and whites outside the South." Clinton got 70 percent of the black vote in Illinois and carried the white vote. But he split the suburban vote with Tsongas in Illinois and, Schneider added, ran "weakest among well-educated and affluent voters." This, Schneider said, could be a problem for Clinton in the presidential election, "because this is going to be the first election for President in which a majority of the voters live in the suburbs."

Tsongas's record as a vote-getter among suburbanites seemed sure to keep him campaigning. His next test was in Connecticut, where he presumably had strength as a New Englander and a man popular in suburbia. But on the eve of the Connecticut primary he abruptly quit. "The hard fact," he said, "is that the nomination process requires resources….We simply did not have the resources." Translated, that meant he did not have enough money to fight in the high-priced media markets of Connecticut and New York.

Clinton moved into Connecticut as the all-but-crowned Democratic standard-bearer. Campaigning in New London, he denounced the Bush plan to kill the locally based, 11,000-job Seawolf nuclear submarine program. His Seawolf endorsement got him an endorsement from the 8,500-member Metal Trades Council in New London.

Brown scoffed at Clinton's support of the Seawolf as pandering while he roamed the state continuing his "We the People" crusade, sleeping in supporters' homes rather than in hotels, accepting $100 checks, and promoting his 800 number. To the surprise of everybody, Brown narrowly beat Clinton in Connecticut. The Democratic primary campaign continued to be a two-man race—but now the two men were Clinton and Brown.

IN THE

CHAPTER 6

CRUCIBLE OF

NEW YORK

BROWN TRUMPETED his one-point triumph in Connecticut as a call to arms against Clinton, his character, and his agenda. "I think it's the people taking politics back into their hands," Brown told CNN anchor Susan Rook. "We gave them a choice....It's going to spread across this country....I see it as a rising up of the people...saying, 'Let's have a politics that's honest, that can work, that cares.'"

CNN's Schneider saw a similar message in exit polls. Voters were asked whether they were satisfied with the candidates. "There were a lot of angry voters in Connecticut," Schneider observed. "And a clear majority said they'd like to see someone else run for President." One of the reasons that Clinton lost: almost half of the surveyed voters "doubted that he had the

Jerry Brown campaigns in midtown Manhattan.

honesty and integrity to serve effectively as President." More than 70 percent said they agreed with Brown's criticism of the political system. Through a volatile political chemistry involving change and character, the system was on trial.

It would be in the crucible of New York City where the next battle would be fought. Brown positioned himself as the liberal alternative and accurately, if existentially, described his role: "We have moved from the media black hole of non-existence to the status of wild card."

Clinton, who had endured so much in so many places in his fight for the nomination now had come to the city where ethnics and economics were in endless struggle, the city where the homeless and the helpless confronted the unheeding rich and the indifferent middle class. Here traditional Democratic liberalism still lived. But so did the pragmatism of party leaders who wanted to win the White House. New York State was Buffalo and Rochester, Albany and Schenectady, dairy farms and endangered aircraft plants. But the real battleground was New York City.

Clinton stood one night in what looked like a cease-fire zone on that battleground, a nightclub in midtown Manhattan, where he was speaking to the faithful who had gathered to give him money. In the midst of Clinton's speech, a member of ACT UP, an AIDS activism organization, heckled

Clinton visits with New York politicians Carol Bellamy (left) and Ruth Messinger.

persistently, and Clinton finally erupted. All the weeks of grinning and handshaking and set speeches faded away and real words tumbled out in a hoarse, raw voice:

"Let me tell you something....I'm fighting to change this country. And let me tell you something else.... You do not have the right to treat any human being, including me, with no respect because of what you're worried about. I did not cause it. I'm trying to do something about it. I have treated you and all the people who've interrupted my rally with a hell of a lot more respect than you've treated me...."

Clinton veered off. He swiped at Jerry Brown "and all the rest of these people who say whatever sounds good at the moment....I'm sick and tired of all these people who don't know me, know nothing about my life, know nothing about the battles that I've fought, know nothing about the life I've lived, making snotty-nose remarks about how I haven't done anything in my life and it's all driven ambition. That's bull, and I'm tired of it."

Clinton's ACT UP blow-up got mixed reviews from New York's 24-hour-a-day media, covering the Clinton-Brown battle as if it were a mob turf war. His flareup showed an anger and resentment that his cool, down-home demeanor had long concealed. Although he directed his wrath toward a heckler, he was also berating the media for focusing on his character and not on the issues he delivered to the campaign.

The Clinton character issue would not go away. Now came accusations that he had weakened Arkansas ethics legislation to benefit himself and his wife. Clinton denied this, just as he had denied prejudice after being caught playing golf at an all-white Little Rock country club, and denied having inhaled when he was asked whether he had once smoked marijuana. TV comics made "I didn't inhale" the Clinton joke of the week.

At a New York City fund-raiser, Brown said he felt "the higher self taking back what belongs to all of us." The remark reminded listeners of Brown's earlier tag: "Governor Moonbeam." His current proposal for a flat tax was criticized as hokus-pokus. Brown would abolish Social Security and gasoline taxes and replace them with a 13 percent tax on income and a 13 percent value-added tax, which, in effect was a national sales tax. Brown claimed that his tax plan was simpler and fairer than the morass that taxpayers slogged through. Critics said the proposal would substantially increase the taxes of the poorest taxpayers and cut in half the taxes of the richest.

Brown, running on his record as a pro-union, pro-poor governor of California, was thumped hard on the flat tax issue. Senator Daniel P.

Clinton became the butt of cartoon humor when he protested that, while he had smoked marijuana, he did not inhale.

Moynihan of New York said the proposal "would put a silver bullet through the heart of Social Security." The flat tax died in the crossfire of the New York primary, but the sniping became fierce enough to threaten Clinton's candidacy also. Brown hammered at Clinton's all-white golf clubbing and his civil-rights record, hoping to hurt him in New York's black precincts.

If Brown defeated Clinton in New York, Clinton might be mortally wounded as a national candidate. New York was that important. "Something destructive is happening in the Democratic presidential campaign," Tom Harkin said, endorsing Clinton and urging labor to support him.

Both candidates went after minority voters, Brown aiming at Jesse Jackson's old rainbow coalition and Clinton looking toward the Jewish vote, which he had lost to Brown in Connecticut. Brown said he would pick Jackson for his running mate, a move that lost him considerable Jewish support. Jews had not forgotten that Jackson, during his 1984 presidential campaign, had called New York City "Hymietown."

As the April 7 New York vote grew closer, Brown got a little boost with a win in Vermont, where Clinton had not campaigned. Meanwhile, Clinton sent Maxine Waters, a black California Congresswoman and friend of Jackson, into the city's black districts. Barney Frank, an openly gay Massachusetts Congressman, spoke to a group of AIDS activists.

A poll on April 5 showed Clinton leading Brown, but about half of the Democrats surveyed said they would just as soon vote for "none of the above." When the votes were counted, Clinton won a resounding victory. Brown came in third behind the drop-out Tsongas. Clinton also won Kansas, Wisconsin, and a non-binding primary in Minnesota.

Exit polls showed that Brown's message did not get through. About 70 percent agreed with him that the system had gone bad, but his flat tax turned voters away. About half of New York's pro-Tsongas voters, according to a CNN poll, voted for Tsongas "not because they liked him but because they disliked the other candidates. A lot of the Tsongas vote was obviously motivated by dislike for Bill Clinton and for Brown."

Clinton carried the voters' uneasiness with him through state after state, consistently winning and slowly erasing the doubts that he could be elected President. His primary campaign was anticlimactic after New York.

End Run Around the Media

Television in 1992 brought viewers a new anti-media game that combines end runs with catching softballs. Ross Perot began the game when he announced his bid for President on "Larry King Live." He kept popping up on talk shows, hurling answers without catching many questions. George Bush and Bill Clinton learned the game quickly, making the rounds of talk shows, getting messages across, avoiding reporters.

Clinton tooted a saxophone on the Arsenio Hall Show, talked with young viewers on MTV, took questions from listeners on NBC's "Today" show, and chatted on "Donahue." When a spokesman for Bush said his talk-show circuit would not include Hall, the late-night host disinvited "George Herbert, irregular-heart-beating, read-my-lipping, slipping-in-the-polls, do-nothing, deficit-raising...sushi-puking Bush." Talk show hosts, unlike reporters, can make speeches.

CLINTON TALKS WITH
COLLEGE-AGE VOTERS.

Michael K. Deaver, President Reagan's former deputy chief of staff, told The New York Times he believed the end-run strategy recognized that talk shows "have become the track the disenfranchised now uses to express its will. The elite press is part of the establishment, as far as the public is concerned...." Washington Post reporter Ruth Marcus was skeptical, "If you have a choice between taking the question from Louise from Omaha or from any reporter, you're going to take Louise from Omaha."

He was clearly the candidate late in April, when rioting flared in Los Angeles. In a triumphant hero's return to the Democratic Leadership Council, he spoke as the Democrats' certain nominee. In his most slashing attack on Bush and the Republicans, Clinton said Bush did not try to heal Los Angeles or to solve the real problems.

When the 1988 Reagan-Bush ticket "needed to prove Michael Dukakis was soft on crime," Clinton said, they brought out Willie Horton. Now, Clinton said, the Republicans "needed to cover up their senseless economic

Commercials

C NN correspondent Brooks Jackson keeps watch on political commercials. During the early primaries, Jackson singled out an ad by Paul Tsongas in which he ran what was supposed to be a Washington Post headline. Tsongas had opposed the Gulf War, so he did not want the war mentioned in his commercial. The alteration was seemingly slight—from the actual headline, "Bush Popularity Surges With Gulf Victory" to "Bush Popularity Surges to 90%." But, as Jackson said, Tsongas "retouched the truth to make the point."

Jackson compared a 1988 commercial showing Vice President George Bush in a flag factory with a 1992 New Hampshire commercial that showed Iowa Senator Tom Harkin in an empty factory. "In this commercial Harkin makes no statement of fact, no specific promises," Jackson pointed out. He also noted the "soft

BUSH ASSOCIATES HIMSELF WITH PATRIOTIC EMBLEMS IN THIS COMMERCIAL.

visual texture" of the Harkin commercial—a sure tipoff that the candidate was aiming at emotion rather than reason.

Jackson noted similar "emotional symbols" in a commercial telecast by Nebraska Senator Bob Kerrey. He is shown at a hockey net, symbolizing the toughness of a goalie. The symbolism carries the emotion more than Kerrey's words, which are as vague as Harkin's were in the empty factory.

Early in the campaign both Democrats and Republicans promised that they strategy," and so they "blame it on quotas so there can be racial resentment instead of honest analysis of our economic falsehoods."

By the time the California primary came in June, Brown no longer was a rival. The state where Brown had governed for eight years gave him second place behind Clinton. The man from Arkansas was ready to accept his party's nomination and finally to take on George Bush. But, with startling swiftness, the politics of the presidential year changed. There was a third man in the race.

would fight clean. But the primary season had hardly started before the first attack ad aired. Conservative Patrick J. Buchanan, challenging President Bush, ran a 30-second commercial that showed a snip from a film in which gay black men in chains and leather dance with each other. An announcer says, "The Bush Administration has wasted our tax dollars on pornographic and blasphemous art." The suggestion was that the National Endowment for the Arts, under Bush, had financed the film. In fact, an organization partially supported by the NEA had partially financed it—and it had happened under Buchanan's hero, President Ronald Reagan.

In half a minute, Buchanan had hit the hot-button issues of pornography, homosexuality, and race. And Buchanan also managed to focus voter ire on a handy target of many of his supporters, the NEA. Using the commercial as a springboard, Buchanan increased criticism of the arts organization, which he called "the upholstered playpen of the arts-and-crafts auxiliary of the Eastern liberal establishment."

BUCHANAN'S COMMERCIAL BASHES THE NEA.

This first attack commercial was also the first to draw blood. Soon after the ad began appearing, Bush forced the resignation of John E. Frohnmayer as chairman of NEA. Judging from the rhetoric of both conventions, commercials are likely to become more vitriolic.

THE THIRD

MAN

CHAPTER 7

PEROT? H. ROSS PEROT? *Who?* In March, a CNN/USA *Today* poll of registered voters had shown that 55 percent of them had never heard of him. But the point was not that a man named Perot had appeared. The point was that voters in the primaries were trying to vote for change, and change was not on the ballot.

By the time of the California primary, Perot news had eclipsed news of Clinton and Bush. On one day in *The Washington Post* there were six pieces on Perot compared to one on Clinton. Perot was the election story of the day, if not the century. Not since Teddy Roosevelt's Bull Moose Party had an independent risen so high, and no independent candidate had ever risen so swiftly.

Yet Perot was not a candidate in California or anywhere else. Officially, he was no one's nominee. He had started the boom himself, with his own words, tossed in a casual way, back in February. Two days after Tsongas won the New Hampshire primary, Perot went on "Larry King Live." At the opening of the show, King reported, "About a third of the voters in New Hampshire's primary said that they wished somebody else were running, and some undoubtedly have this guy in mind."

King leaned across the table and asked, "Are you going to run?"

Ross Perot, an American success story, attracted grassroots support.

"No," Perot replied.

"Flat 'no'?" King persisted.

Perot sidestepped, saying, "But we've got an hour tonight to talk about the real problems that face this nation. And you, in effect, have sort of an electronic town hall, so I think we can serve the country by really getting down in the trenches, talking about what we have to do, and then doing it."

And so it went for several minutes, King pushing for a commitment, Perot uttering can-do lines: "jump-start the economy," "link arms and work together," stop the "mud wrestling" between Congress and the White House, develop "a strong family unit in every home."

The discussion veered to Japan ("our rival, not our enemy") and what is wrong with American corporations ("If you've got a losing team, you start with the coach, right?"). Listeners began calling in with questions about taxes and jobs and government bureaucracy. Toward the end of the show, King abruptly changed subjects, "By the way, is there any scenario in which you would run for President?"

Perot said he did not want to run for President.

"I know," King said. "But is there a scenario?"

Perot stalled, and King asked him again if there were a scenario.

He said he would not run as either a Democrat or a Republican, "because I will not sell out to anybody but to the American people—and I will sell out to them."

"So you'd run as an independent?"

"...If you're that serious—you, the people, are that serious—you register me in 50 states, and if you're not willing to organize and do that—"

"Wait a minute!" King cut in. "Are you saying—? Wait a minute."

"—then this is all just talk."

"Hold it! Hold it! Hold it! Hold it!" King yelled.

"Now stay with me, Larry—"

"Wait! Wait! Are you saying—?"

"I'm saying to the ordinary folks—now I don't want any machine....I'm saying to all these nice people that have written to me—and the letters, you know, fill cases—if you're dead serious—"

"Start committees," King broke in.

"—then I want to see some sweat—"

It went on like that, a string of interrupted phrases, until Perot made a long speech full of incredibly mixed metaphors about putting on the gloves and climbing a cliff and then climbing out of the ring and staying in the fight and registering him in 50 states, and then Perot finally said, "I don't want any money from anybody but you, and I don't want anything but five bucks from you because I can certainly pay for my own campaign—no ifs, ands, and buts. But I want you to have skin in the game. I want you to be in the ring. . . .The shoe is on the other foot."

With that cliché mysteriously ending his acceptance speech, H. Ross Perot was in the campaign. The *H* (for Henry) would shortly disappear, as would Perot's bashfulness about being a presidential candidate.

Although the byplay on the Larry King show had been spontaneous, the thinking behind it had been as deliberate and calculating as a Perot bid for a corporate merger. Talk about Perot as a presidential candidate had been buzzing for years. Back in 1987, for example, after Perot spoke before the National Governors' Association, the chairman of the association suggested that Perot run for President. The chairman was Arkansas Governor Bill Clinton.

In November 1991, Tennessee Democrat John Jay Hooker called Perot and suggested that a Perot-for-President movement get started. Early in February 1992, Perot, at Hooker's urging, met with a group of Nashville

On CNN's "Larry King Live" show, the host prodded Perot into his first national public declaration of intent.

movers and shakers. A business woman in the audience asked him about running, and the next day *The Tennessean,* Nashville's major newspaper, published his answer, "If you feel so strongly about this, register me in 50 states. If it's 49, forget it. If you want to do 50 states, you care that much, fine, then I don't belong to anybody but you."

The remarks rehearsed what he told King two weeks later, but, on the King show, the words produced an immediate result. In Dallas the day after Perot's chat with Larry King, the switchboard of Perot's company stopped working because of an overload of calls. A 100-line telephone bank was quickly installed and—à la Jerry Brown—an 800 number was set up. Volunteers, overseen by Perot employees, began handling calls at the rate of 90,000 an hour. According to Perot, his 800 number was the busiest in telephone history.

By March 5, Tennesseans had signed enough petitions to qualify Perot for the presidential election, making the state the first to have him officially entered on the November ballot. Six weeks after his demand for a 50-state groundswell, there were Perot volunteer organizations in every state. Hundreds of thousands of volunteers transformed the presidential campaign into a three-way race.

In Florida, with a former Vietnam POW in charge, 20,000 volunteers

Perot volunteers came from a middle class that felt disenfranchised.

signed up within the first hour of the first day. In Iowa, where 1,000 signatures were needed, volunteers collected more than 100,000. On June 18, Perot's movement, as people were calling it, announced that it had amassed 1,408,708 signatures on petitions to put him on state ballots. By July 1, volunteers had submitted petitions to 32 states, and notifications of Perot's presence on the ballot were coming in, state by state.

His supporters came from across the political spectrum. One poll showed him getting a third of his support from conservatives, another third from moderates, and a third from liberals. "Everybody is making him up," a political commentator said, "believing that he is whatever you wish he might be." Near the end of April the Texas Poll showed Perot leading both Bush and Clinton in that state. A CNN/USA Today poll in June had him getting more than half of all independents and 42 percent of moderates. The core of the middle class—voters with family incomes between $30,000 and $50,000—favored him over both Bush and Clinton.

More than half the voters said they knew little or nothing about him. That was the most amazing aspect of an amazing phenomenon: no one knew his specific plans for bringing about change. The media, drawn to this new element in the race, at first concentrated on a biographical look at Perot, essentially publishing or broadcasting his resumé. He had been an Eagle Scout, the president of his class at the U.S. Naval Academy, a champion IBM salesman, an entrepreneur who started his own company with $1,000 and became a billionaire. As to his character, he was a Texan with a mind of his own and his own way of doing things.

When he did not feel IBM paid enough attention to the ideas of a star salesman, he founded a computer firm called Electronic Data Systems in Dallas. He made money and shaped a talented work force to his image. EDS men could sprout neatly trimmed mustaches but not beards. Women could not wear pants suits. "I put a strong store on strong moral values," Perot said, vowing to fire any adulterous employee.

The resumé also included his exploits as a patriot. In 1969 he sent Christmas dinners and gifts to prisoners of war in North Vietnam. The POWs did not get the dinners and gifts, but H. Ross Perot became known to the American people as a quirky patriot. Subsequently, he offered to ransom U.S. hostages in Lebanon, organized a rescue mission to free two EDS employees jailed in Iran, and tracked down reports of U.S. servicemen still held prisoner in Vietnam and Laos.

Perot was hailed as a business genius when he sold EDS to General

Motors for $2.55 billion and a place on the GM board. After harassing GM chairman Roger B. Smith and making threats about "nuking the GM system," Perot accepted a $700-million deal to leave his seat on the board and his stake in GM and just go away. He started another company, Perot Systems, stealing executives from EDS.

As a civic reformer, he headed a Texas commission on schools. Paying for his own lobbyists, he pushed through the state legislature a "no pass, no play" rule that gored a Texas sacred cow—high-school football—by forcing boys with bad report cards off the team. He also enraged the teachers' lobby by getting a law that mandated competency examinations for teachers.

So that was Ross Perot: All-American boy, patriot, business genius (who got his inspiration from a book entitled *Leadership Secrets of Attila the Hun*). Actually he was also that terrible thing to be in 1992 politics—an insider—though he tried hard to portray himself otherwise. In fact, he had had White House access from Lyndon B. Johnson to George Bush.

When EDS had a problem during the Nixon Administration with a federal contract to process Medicare claims in Texas, Perot went directly to Robert H. Finch, Secretary of Health, Education, and Welfare. When Marine Lt. Col. Oliver North was raising funds to ransom U.S. hostages as part of the Reagan Administration's Iran-Contra scheme, $200,000 in cash from Perot was one of the items in North's famous White House safe. Fellow Texan Perot also was an old friend of George Bush.

But that friendship changed when Perot became a potential candidate against Bush. Stung by reports that Perot had "investigated" members of the Bush family, the President said, "I'm sick about it if it's true....And I think the American people will reject that kind of tactic." Perot said he had merely tipped off Bush, father to father, about a deal that one of Bush's sons had almost become involved in. Perot then embarrassed the President by releasing a handwritten note from Bush thanking Perot for his help.

The Bush Administration drumbeat against Perot continued. Vice President Dan Quayle set the tone of a Perot-is-a-dangerous-man campaign: "Imagine having the IRS, the FBI, and CIA under his control." Quayle also called him a "temperamental tycoon with contempt for the Constitution." Drug czar Bob Martinez chimed in with, "This nation didn't gain a hard-won victory in the cold war only to surrender its constitutional liberties to a secretive computer salesman." Press Secretary Marlin

The contradiction of a populist billionaire was obvious to political commentators.

Fitzwater used the words "monster" and "dangerous" to describe Perot.

Perot continued campaigning on talk shows, following a 1992 trend by chatting on "20/20" and the "Phil Donahue Show." He made wisecracks and needled the administration. But he did not lay out any position papers or step forth with well-considered policies. He was fond of saying he would get people together in a room and hammer out a solution. His was a CEO's view of how to settle a board-room squabble.

After being questioned sharply at the American Society of Newspaper Editors convention, Perot said, "I'm not driven to do this. Matter of fact, the more I'm in it, the less interesting it becomes." The statement was prophetic, as was his answer to CNN anchor Bernard Shaw, who asked, "If you are so pumped up about change in leadership at the top, why have you ducked the real acid test, the primaries and the caucuses?" Perot replied, "I have no desire to be in political life. I've said for years when people try to get me to run that I'm a businessman. If I have a purpose in life, it's to create jobs and taxpayers. I'm action-oriented."

Perot hoped to run a non-campaign, making it up as he went along, dodging or pummeling the media, not saying that he was, indeed, a candidate. He finally realized that he needed to call in professionals, but insisted, "I'll be my own person....They will not be my handlers...."

The non-handlers he hired were Edward J. Rollins, the manager of

Ronald Reagan's 1984 reelection campaign, and Hamilton Jordan, who ran Jimmy Carter's successful presidential campaign in 1976 and his unsuccessful campaign four years later. With both a Republican and a Democratic professional working for him, Perot strengthened his independent, non-politician image.

Rollins pushed Perot to lay out his programs. Perot resisted the advice. Shown raw film for proposed commercials, Perot, who had little respect for advertising, turned them down and suggested that he could keep getting free television, as he had from Larry King, Barbara Walters, and "Today." He did not seem to understand that he had to campaign to be elected President.

On July 11, Perot appeared in Nashville before the convention of the NAACP. Aides worried because he would be speaking before the first audience not organized by his campaign. But he turned down suggestions about what he should say and gave his standard, rambling speech, throwing in condescending remarks about his father's dealings, as a smalltown cotton-broker, with black men and women. He referred to the African Americans in the audience as "you people." Yet, in the storm of criticism that followed, Perot was surprised that the NAACP delegates had been offended.

The day after the NAACP speech, Rollins handed Perot a memo suggesting plans for what Perot had promised his followers, "a world-class campaign." Rollins said that Perot had to start the campaign immediately to have any chance of winning. Perot rejected the plan. Rollins then wrote another memo—his last—saying that Perot had three choices: run a real campaign, stumble through a losing non-campaign, or quit.

On July 17, while Bill Clinton was in New York City preparing to receive his party's nomination, Perot topped the news about the Democrats by announcing that he was quitting as a candidate for President. Perot told a news conference that he "just rationally looked at the facts" and decided that, because he could not win in November, the election would probably be decided in the House of Representatives. And, since the House is made up of Democrats and Republicans, "our group would be unlikely to win."

Most people familiar with Perot's 147 days in politics believed that he had quit because he had learned to hate politics. He had rejected the traditional organization and tactics of a presidential campaign. Tom Johnson, the president of CNN, after speaking with Perot, said Perot "conveyed strong feelings of anguish about the process." At one point,

Johnson said, Perot complained, "They've attacked me on everything in the world."

When Perot withdrew, his name was on the ballot in 18 states: Alabama, Alaska, Arkansas, Colorado, Florida, Idaho, Kansas, Kentucky, Maine, Massachusetts, Nebraska, New Hampshire, North Carolina, Tennessee, Texas, Utah, Washington, and Wyoming. In six other states—California, Delaware, Montana, Nevada, New Jersey, and Oklahoma—he had taken the steps necessary to qualify but was not yet officially on the ballot. "What he's done isn't right," reacted one volunteer. But she and tens of thousands like her still planned to vote for him. "This movement," another volunteer said, "is going to be around forever."

Perot could have had his name removed from nearly all the ballots just by mailing a letter to state officials. But he continued to encourage his supporters, urging them to keep gathering signatures in states where his name had not yet been put on the ballot. Volunteer organizations claimed by late August to have Perot entered in 48 states.

Coming full circle, Perot appeared on "Larry King Live" the night after his announcement that he was out of the race. Or was he? "I explained yesterday," he told King in a slightly exasperated tone, "that I was still on the ballot. And I thought that they could extrapolate from there. But I guess I should have detailed it out more."

As he attempted to do that during the interview, confusion spiraled higher than it had the day before. King, looking uncharacteristically baffled, asked if Perot were trying to create a protest vote of his followers while staying off the ticket himself. Perot gave no direct answer. He mentioned the campaign ads that had been prepared before he quit. The ads, he said, "are in the can. So no problem there. And they are killers."

"Wait a minute," King demanded. If you're not dead in October, would you run these?"

"No. No. The point is, if you have to tap both presidential candidates on the shoulder. Say, 'Look, guys, if you force us to, then we have an exit here. We've got an option.' But, for God's sake, let's make the system work and put tremendous pressure on the system to make it work, and then get action next year."

So the Perot movement ended with the same ambiguity as it had begun. But the force that had so swiftly uplifted Perot was not the thrust of the man. It was the drive for change, the repulsion voters were feeling toward the kind of politics their politicians were giving them.

AGENTS

OF

CHAPTER 8

CHANGE

BY AUGUST THE IDEA of change was everywhere. At the Republican convention, Bush tried to mold change into a theme he could ride. Beyond America, the Bush Years were the "Fast Years," a time when the Cold War melted away, when the Soviet Union fell apart, when democracy surged across eastern Europe, when the two Germanys reunited. "If I had stood before you four years ago and described this as the world we would help build," Bush said in his acceptance speech, "you would have said, 'George Bush, you must be smoking something, and you must have inhaled.'"

He paid his respects to change, but the touch of Jim Baker was evident, too. "This election is about change," Bush said. "But that's not unusual,

Jim Baker leaves the State Department for the White House to aid Bush campaign.

because the American revolution is never ending. Today, the pace of change is accelerating. We face new opportunities and new challenges. And the question is: who do you trust to make change work for you?"

That was the twist, from change to trust. "Sure, we must change, but some values are timeless. I believe in families...." To trust, Bush added "traditional family values," a vague issue that he would try to harden into the dominant theme of the campaign, a theme that would challenge the character and values not only of Bill Clinton but also of his wife and of the Americans who supported the Clinton quest for change.

One month earlier, Ross Perot's withdrawal gave Bill Clinton a new paragraph for his acceptance speech, a welcome to the Perot volunteers: "I am well aware that those who rallied in his cause wanted to enlist in an army of patriots for change. We say to them: join us. Together we will revitalize America." That was one of the words Perot used when he tried to explain why he had quit. "The Democratic Party has revitalized itself," Perot said.

A feeling of vitality did surge through Clinton's speech and through Madison Square Garden when he accepted his nomination. He was back in New York City, where he had fought his toughest primary battle. And he knew why those Democrats out there had chosen him. Above all else, Clinton had offered change, and revitalize was the synonym of the moment.

"Our values—freedom, democracy, individual rights, and free enterprise—they have triumphed all around the world," Clinton said. "And yet, just as we have won the Cold War abroad, we are losing the battles for economic opportunity and social justice here at home. Now that we have changed the world, it's time to change America. I have news for the forces of greed and the defenders of the status quo: your time has come and gone. It's time for a change in America."

It had become time for change in the Democratic Party, too, a time to find new routes to victory. No longer were cities where the votes were. Smoldering Los Angeles had become a symbol of the American city of the 1990s—a place of despair and crime, poverty and rage. At a time when cities needed more help than ever before, the population shift—the so-called white flight—was giving suburban voters more clout. This transition was reflected in the reapportionment of voting districts for Congress and state legislatures.

In Philadelphia, for example, the percentage of non-white population rose from about 35 percent in 1970 to about 48 percent in 1990. The city

Bill Clinton walks through a section of the Los Angeles riot area with Representative Maxine Waters and other black leaders.

lost more than 102,000 residents between 1980 and 1990. Two of the city's congressional districts became suburban. Similarly, New York City's share of the state's congressional delegation dropped from 51 percent in 1960 to 41 percent in 1992.

Clinton could turn his strategy away from cities, but he could not ignore them. He had to solve a complex political problem. He had to show sympathy and compassion, especially toward the most loyal of Democrats, the black voters. But he could not woo African Americans so aggressively that he antagonized the blue-collar and middle-class voters soured on entitlements and affirmative action issues.

The quickest way for Clinton to accomplish this was to humble Jesse Jackson. The proud black leader had made highly publicized demands upon Walter Mondale in 1984 and upon Michael Dukakis in 1988 before campaigning for either candidate. Now Clinton, determined not to become beholden to Jackson, had to find a way to defy him without alienating blacks and others in Jackson's Rainbow Coalition.

Jackson, named by Jerry Brown as a potential running mate, had frowned on Clinton's selection of Senator Al Gore of Tennessee as his candidate for Vice President. Jackson had said that, with two southerners, the ticket did not have enough diversity, and he could not immediately

Jesse Jackson appears at the Democratic National Convention after endorsing the two-southerner ticket of Bill Clinton and Al Gore.

accept it. Clinton had not taken the bait. "He'll just have to make up his own mind on that, like every American," Clinton said.

Shortly before the Democratic convention, Clinton found his opportunity to distance himself from Jackson. Clinton was invited to address a Rainbow convention in Washington. Black rap singer Sister Souljah was also on the program. The little-known rapper had been catapulted to notoriety when, shortly after the Los Angeles riots, *The Washington Post* had quoted her as saying, "If black people kill black people every day, why not have a week and kill white people?...So, if you're a gang member and you would normally be killing somebody, why not kill a white person?"

When Clinton stepped to the podium, Jackson and his followers expected a soothing sermon on equality and an endorsement of Jackson's 10-year, trillion-dollar "plan to rebuild America." Instead, Clinton chastized Sister Souljah for words that were "filled with the kind of hatred that you"—Jackson and the coalition—"do not honor today." Jackson glowered at the head table.

Later, Jackson, scowling and infuriated, told a press conference that Clinton "came to that meeting with a ploy." He had seen through the ploy, he said, when he learned that Clinton's aides had alerted the media to cover the speech. "I did not pounce on him when he was down," Jackson added, perhaps inadvertently describing his own status in the Democratic Party. "I reached out to him, similar to his playing golf at the country club....This is not a slip of the lip. This is a plan....It was a ploy for division, at a time when we need healing."

But few were listening to Jackson. If he expected an apology from Clinton, he got none. And, a few days before the Democratic convention, Jackson endorsed Clinton. Times had changed.

If change had driven Clinton's primary campaign, it had also become the dominant buzz word by the time of the Democratic and Republican conventions. But issues were what the 1992 presidential election was supposed to be about, and the issues—whatever they were—seemed to be getting lost in the chants about change.

"Change: from what to what?" asked former Representative Barbara Jordan in an emotional address at the Democratic convention. She spoke movingly of the American dream "slipping away from too many black and brown mothers and their children; from the homeless of every color and sex; from the immigrants living in communities without water and sewer systems." But the change that she saw had hard edges, and it spoke to the central theme of the convention: the changing of the Democratic Party itself, "from a party with a reputation of tax and spend to one of investment and growth. A growth economy is a must," she counseled.

With investment and growth, Jordan had not sounded the old-time Democratic anthem. The Democrats, like the Republicans, were talking about economic growth rather than promising to share America's wealth.

Barbara Jordan of Texas, a Democratic icon, calls on convention delegates to change the party itself.

VALUES AS

ISSUES

WHEN THE 107 MEMBERS of the Republican platform committee reached a phrase in the final draft describing America as "the last best hope for man on earth," a man spoke up. He said he was a Christian, and he knew that the last best hope of man was Jesus Christ. That, he argued, was what the platform should say. After a 30-minute discussion, the committee finally decided to keep the Lincolnian phrase.

In the 95-page platform that President Bush and Vice President Quayle stand on, every phrase, every word was candled against the torch of truth as held by conservatives. Rarely was the voice of a Republican moderate heard. Even the President was censured in an early draft that called his 1990 tax increase a "mistake." A presidential adviser got the committee to remove the word, though Bush obligingly said in his acceptance speech, "it was a mistake."

The Christian Coalition, created by the Reverend Pat Robertson, 1988 presidential candidate and TV evangelist, claimed 20 members and 8 allies on the platform committee. Robertson's followers were so influential that they erased one of Bush's favorite expressions, "new world order." Robertson had co-opted the phrase in his 1991 book, *The New World Order*. Bush and other leaders, by fostering a one-world government,

George Bush, accepting renomination, asks, "Who do you trust to make change work?"

Bush tells Republicans: "Our policies haven't failed, they haven't been tried."

Robertson wrote, were "unknowingly and unwittingly carrying out the mission and mouthing the phrases of a tightly knit cabal whose goal is nothing less than a new world order for the human race under the domination of Lucifer and his followers." A spokesman for Robertson said that the cabal's phrase, "new world order," would not appear in the Republican platform and would not be used anymore by Bush. Robertson also sees a feminist plot. In a letter to Iowans who will vote on an Equal Rights Amendment to the state constitution, Robertson said that the "feminist agenda" is "a socialist, anti-family political movement that encourages women to leave their husbands, kill their children, practice witchcraft, destroy capitalism, and become lesbians."

Another ghostwriter hovering over the platform was conservative presidential candidate Patrick Buchanan. On the primary trail, he had urged that the United States build a wall or dig a trench along the Rio Grande to keep out illegal Mexican immigrants. The Republican platform gives Buchanan his wall, though it is camouflaged as "structures necessary to secure the border."

The Bush Administration, currently negotiating a trade agreement with Mexico and reaching out to Latino voters, did not like the border "structures" any more than it liked an abortion plank that went beyond

Bush's own stand on the issue. But the Bush wing accepted it all. "We couldn't have written most of this ourselves in a stronger fashion," said Bay Buchanan, Pat's sister and campaign manager.

"Traditional family values," a refrain of the religious right, became a key campaign theme. Bush worked a values line into his standard stump speech: we must "make our families more like the Waltons and a little bit less like the Simpsons," meaning, of course, more like Republicans than Democrats. A hand-lettered sign on the convention floor decoded the phrase in another way: "Woody Allen, family values adviser to Bill Clinton."

The Republican platform, under the heading "Uniting Our Family," says, "The culture of our Nation has traditionally supported...personal responsibility, morality, and the family." Three paragraphs later, the platform says, "Moreover, we oppose efforts by the Democrat (sic) Party to include sexual preference as a protected minority receiving preferential status under civil rights statutes at the federal, State, and local level. We oppose any legislation or law which legally recognizes same-sex marriages and allows such couples to adopt children or provide foster care." The Democratic Party platform calls for "civil rights protection for gay men and lesbians and an end to Defense Department discrimination." There is no mention of same-sex marriages.

Usually, party platforms are merely anthems to party principles and draw little attention. But this year the platforms pointed up differences that define the changes in the parties—toward the center for the Democrats, far to the right for the Republicans. And nowhere was difference more apparent than on the issue of abortion.

Clinton hammers hard at this issue that most divides the parties, their platforms and their candidates. But, like many politicians in both parties, he wishes the issue would go away. "I hope," he says, "we never have another campaign for the President where what ought to be a personal and painful and private decision is the subject of platform speeches because politicians are trying to take away the woman's right to choose."

Delegates going into the Houston Astrodome for the Republican National Convention saw a billboard dominated by a big "71." That was the percentage of Republicans who were pro-choice, according to a recent poll. The billboard was one attempt to eclipse the platform, which called for a constitutional amendment banning abortions and added, "We believe the unborn child has a fundamental right to life which cannot be infringed."

Mary Dent Crisp, leader of the National Coalition for Choice, said to television cameras, "My party is sending the message to women, 'Be quiet and go away.' "

Bush got his chance to sidle away from the platform when he was asked in an NBC "Dateline" interview whether he would support a granddaughter who wanted an abortion. "Of course, I'd stand by my child," he replied. "I'd love her and help her." He said he would try to talk her out of it, but, ultimately, the decision would be hers. "Well, whose else's—who else's—could it be?" he asked. Vice President Dan Quayle, asked a similar question on "Larry King Live," said he would support his teenage daughter if she, as an adult, chose to have an abortion. But his wife, Marilyn, said, "If she becomes pregnant, she'll take the child to term." Barbara Bush told interviewers that abortion is a "personal decision." Like Clinton, she believed that abortion should not be mentioned in a political platform.

Pro-choice advocates gleefully claimed that two Bushes and one Quayle had become converts. A woman for choice walked around the GOP convention in a T-shirt emblazoned "Finally, Barbara." David Keene of the American Conservative Union told The New York Times, "If just Quayle has said something, you could look at it as an accident. But with three comments like that in succession, you know it's a deliberate plan."

A side issue to the abortion debate is the use of fetal tissue for medical research on such diseases as diabetes, Alzheimer's, leukemia, schizophrenia, and Parkinson's. The Bush Administration has banned federal funding for research using fetal tissue, and in June 1992 Bush vetoed a bill to lift the ban, saying it had "potential for promoting and legitimizing abortion." Though Bush approved setting up banks using tissue from ectopic pregnancies and miscarriages, researchers said there is a continual shortage of such tissue.

In this year's debate, speeches about family values and life styles are getting more attention than speeches about hard-edged issues like the economy and health care and the over-arching theme of change.

"Sure we must change," said the President in his acceptance speech, "but some values are timeless. I believe in families that stick together, and fathers who stick around. I happen to believe very deeply in the worth of each individual human being, born or unborn. And I believe in teaching our kids the difference between what's wrong and what's right, teaching them respect for hard work and to love their neighbors."

Republicans drew a straight line from family values to attacks on Hillary

Clinton. A lawyer who earns more money than her husband, she was also the head of the Children's Defense Fund, an advocacy organization. Buchanan led the attacks on her at the convention, saying, "Hillary believes that 12-year-olds should have a right to sue their parents, and she has compared marriage as an institution to slavery and life on an Indian reservation. . . . Friends, this is radical feminism."

TV cameras switched to Barbara Bush, who was seated next to Buchanan's wife. They both applauded, and after the speech, Buchanan defied protocol by waiting for Barbara Bush to walk over to him to shake his hand, rather than approaching her. She had approved the targeting of Hillary Clinton because she was not just a candidate's wife but also "a self-proclaimed co-President."

Marilyn Quayle, in her speech nominating Bush, took aim at Hillary Clinton and her values, saying that not everyone in their generation "believed that the family was so oppressive that women could only thrive apart from it. . . . Most of us love being mothers or wives." Marilyn Quayle is not only a mother and a wife, but also a first-time novelist and, like Hillary Clinton, a lawyer. But, rhetorically, Marilyn Quayle stood before the convention as a wife and mother.

"They're running against Hillary," Bill Clinton said, ". . . trying to make it a Willie Horton issue." The attacks came as Republican polls showed Hillary Clinton to be more a liability than asset for Bill Clinton.

An article by Hillary Clinton in a 1973 academic journal was the source

Barbara Bush, speaking at the Republican convention, stresses "family values" and reaches out to women in and out of the home. More than half of women voters are in the work force.

Marilyn and Dan Quayle, both of whom stressed values in their convention speeches, listen to President Bush say, "Sure we must change, but some values are timeless."

of Buchanan's charges. The article, in *The Harvard Educational Review*, discussed the evolution of laws involving children: "The basic rationale for depriving people of rights in a dependency relationship is that certain individuals are incapable or undeserving of the right to take care of themselves and consequently need social institutions specifically designed to safeguard their position....Along with the family, past and present examples of such arrangements include marriage, slavery, and the Indian reservation system."

As for Buchanan's allegation about 12-year-olds suing their parents, what she actually wrote in a 1979 article was that major decisions about a child's life "should be resolved by the families, not the courts," except "in all but the most extreme cases." Then, she wrote, "Decisions about motherhood and abortion, schooling, cosmetic surgery, treatment of venereal disease, or employment, and others where the decision or lack of one will significantly affect the child's future, should not be made unilaterally by parents. Children should have a right to be permitted to decide their own future if they are competent." In an era of sound-bite charges and counter-charges, the actual ideas in Hillary Clinton's articles got little media follow-up.

In contrast, Vice President Quayle touched off a vigorous media reaction when he criticized the title character in the "Murphy Brown" TV show. His speech served up one of the first "value" remarks of the campaign. Speaking shortly after the Los Angeles riots, he said, "The intergenerational poverty that troubles us so much today is predominantly a poverty of values....It doesn't help matters when prime-time TV has Murphy Brown—a character who supposedly epitomizes today's intelligent, highly paid professional woman—mocking the importance of fathers by bearing a child alone and calling it just another 'life-style' choice."

Quayle's Murphy Brown remark connected with the media and the public. In a survey of 3,500 Americans, 65 percent were able to identify "Murphy Brown" as the TV program that Dan Quayle had criticized, but only 21 percent answered Yugoslavia when asked which former communist country was engaged in a civil war.

The emergence of values as a major issue came as the end of the Cold War deprived the Republicans of the enduring, if disputable, theme that they were hard on communism and the Democrats were soft. The values theme also diverted voter attention away from economic issues. As Bush began his campaign for a second term, the economy was showing feeble growth. But unemployment was 7.7 percent nationally, was near 10 percent in California, and was chronic in New England and the Rust Belt. The major topic in many states was a phrase all too familiar to Bush: "jobs, jobs, jobs." Secretary of State James Baker had used that very incantation when asked what the Gulf War was all about, and Bush used it to explain his illness-inducing trip to Japan in January 1992.

Another substantive issue, health care, discovered by the Democrats earlier, found its way into Bush's acceptance speech. The issue has been driven by skyrocketing costs and failure of the health-insurance system to reach many who need it. Since Bush entered the White House, the price of medical care has gone up 32 percent, twice the rise in the Consumer Price Index. About 36 million Americans do not have health insurance.

Bush criticized Clinton's plan as "socialized" and "nationalized" and said it lacked both efficiency and compassion. Clinton supporters say Bush's plan "combines the compassion of his anti-recession program with the efficiency of his S&L bailout." Analysts looking at the plans say they both would increase the use of health maintenance organizations and that Bush's plan would probably kill off small insurance firms.

The difference between Clinton and Bush at the beginning of their campaigns is what they hope to make the dominant issues in the campaign. Clinton hopes the voters will focus on the economy and health care. Bush hopes the campaign will revolve around family values. The hopes of both candidates must be translated into strategies, where to find the votes and what to do to get them.

Issues: Abortion, Budget/Deficit Reduction

BUSH and PLATFORM	CLINTON and PLATFORM

Abortion

THEN

As Congressman in the 1960s, encouraged birth control and was the principal Republican author of the 1970 Family Planning Act. As U.S. Ambassador to the UN, promoted reduction of world population growth. Supported abortion rights during 1980 campaign against Reagan, but came out against abortion as Reagan's running mate. As President, appointed two conservative justices to Supreme Court creating a majority that, many fear, will overturn the Roe v. Wade decision.	As Governor of Arkansas, Clinton signed a law requiring girls under 18 to notify a judge or their parents before getting an abortion. Clinton's running mate, Senator Al Gore, as a House member, voted against federal funds to pay for abortions.

NOW

Anti-abortion except in cases of rape or incest or to save the life of the mother (though Republican platform makes no such exceptions). Supports a boycott of the UN Population Fund, the principal family planning organization in 141 developing nations. Wants a constitutional amendment to overthrow Roe v. Wade.	Supports the Freedom of Choice Act, but also wants some restrictions on access to abortion. Has said he will not push for a law allowing Medicaid financing of abortions, but if Congress passes such a bill, he will sign it. The Supreme Court, in its most recent decision on abortion, skirted Roe v. Wade. Clinton says the future of Roe now hinges on swing vote of one justice and that when he has the opportunity he will appoint abortion-rights supporters to the Supreme Court. Backs testing of the French-made abortion pill. Gore is pro-choice.

Budget/Deficit Reduction

THEN

Called for a balanced budget amendment to the Constitution. Raised $146 billion through taxes, required new user fees, or cuts in entitlement programs like Medicare and farm-price supports. His 1990 budget put caps on spending in domestic, international, and defense during FY 1991-93, later to be lumped together under a single cap. "Peace dividend" prohibited by spending "walls" between categories. Caps can be exceeded only if the President and Congress agree to declare a "budget emergency."	His governors' task force in 1990 called for Bush to use "peace dividend" to cut deficit and aid domestic needs.

Issues: Cities, Civil Rights

BUSH and PLATFORM	CLINTON and PLATFORM	
Wants to cut both domestic spending and taxes, change budget accounting, and extend caps through 1997. To keep Congress in check would "require that, for every tax dollar set aside to cut the debt, the ceilings on spending will be cut by an equal amount. That way, we will cut both debt and spending and take a whack out of the budget deficit....We must have new incentives for research and new training for workers. Small businesses need capital and credit, and defense workers need new jobs." Wants line-item veto.	Wants to cut deficit in half across four years by $140 billion-plus spending cuts that would shrink defense expenditures, reform Pentagon procurement, and tighten up other government spending. Opposes Bush's version of balanced budget amendment. Wants line-item veto authority. Would use combination of tax increases and budget cuts to trim deficit. (Platform specifically slashes "federal administrative costs by 3% annually for four years.") Has two plans, one based on moderate and one based on strong economic growth, to cut deficit by half or by 75% by 1996.	**NOW**

Cities

The Administration has examined ideas, such as HUD Secretary Kemp's urban enterprise zones and loans for tenants to buy their public housing units. These have been "in the pipeline" while Bush and Congress, hamstrung by spending caps, grappled with the deficit.	Has little urban-affairs experience as governor of basically rural state. Joined with other governors in giving some support to increased federal-funding demands by big-city mayors.	**THEN**
Supports enterprise zones. Would add $1.1 billion in emergency assistance and small business loans to a supplemental appropriations bill. Backs Kemp's public housing reforms, including tenant ownership.	Would give federally owned housing, including that on closed military bases, to community groups to house the homeless. Encourages resident ownership of lower income housing. Gives cities matching grants for crime-control projects. Creates urban enterprise zones with minimal federal and tax regulations in return for which businesses must employ local residents.	**NOW**

Civil Rights

Attacked Civil Rights Act of 1990 as a "quota bill," but signed it.	Clinton supported a state civil rights law in Arkansas in 1991, but it was not passed by the legislature.	**THEN**

Issues: Drugs/Crime, Defense, Economy

	BUSH and PLATFORM	CLINTON and PLATFORM
N O W	**Civil Rights continued** Platform focuses on protection of "family values" and "equality of opportunity," rather than on civil rights. "Asserting equal rights for all, we support...vigorous enforcement of statutes to prevent illegal discrimination on account of sex, race, creed, or national origin....we reject efforts to replace equal rights with quotas or other preferential treatment."	Platform promises fight "to ensure that no Americans suffer discrimination or deprivation of rights on the basis of race, gender, language, national origin, religion, age, disability, sexual orientation, or other characteristics irrelevant to ability." Backs ERA and affirmative action, rejects "discriminatory English-only pressure groups."

Drugs/Crime

T H E N	Has supported the death penalty and has tried to have habeas corpus laws amended to deny death row prisoners access to federal appeals courts. Drug-war money has gone two-thirds for enforcement, one-third for treatment, education.	Has supported the death penalty. There have been executions during his terms as governor.
N O W	Wants more funding for prisons, death penalty for additional 50 federal crimes. Proposes to continue to spend on drug law enforcement here and abroad.	Supports the death penalty. Will add 100,000 police officers to streets. Create National Police Corps of unemployed veterans.

Defense

T H E N	Claims "Peace Through Strength" won the Cold War. Said in 1992 will continue cuts in spending to a total of 30% ($50 billion) by 1997.	In Democratic Leadership Council, pulled centrists away from the pro-spending views of conservative southerners like Senators Sam Nunn and Charles Robb.
N O W	"We must be a military superpower," but supports "prudent cuts." No military personnel cuts above 25% so as to maintain morale. Wants to keep funding Strategic Defense Initiative ("Star Wars") to stay ahead of tactical weapons like Iraqi Scuds.	Wants 30% cut, while maintaining a "survivable nuclear force to deter any conceivable threat." Use military research facilities for domestic projects. Cut back U.S. troops in Europe. Stop production of B2 bomber, continue production of Seawolf submarine.

Economy

T H E N	Continued supply-side economics of the Reagan Administration. Until late 1991, insisted nation was not in recession. Argued that if Congress had done as he	As chairman of centrist Democratic Leadership Council backed non-liberal ideas: tax credits instead of minimum-wage hikes for working poor; incentives

BUSH and PLATFORM	CLINTON and PLATFORM	
asked and lowered capital gains tax and passed other measures to stimulate economy, recession could have been avoided. Since acknowledging recession, his Administration pressured Federal Reserve to lower interest rates to stimulate spending and called on Congress to pass series of proposals designed to stimulate economy.	for savings and productivity rather than expansion of government aid for poor. Led governors in rejection of "the old economic debate, Sunbelt versus Frostbelt," arguing that "economy as a whole suffers" if any region has financial problems.	**THEN**
Platform supports "increased access to capital for business expansion, exporting, long-term investment, opportunity capital for the disadvantaged, and capital to bring new products and new technology to the market."	Rebuild America Fund with $20 billion federal investment each year for four years, leveraged with state, local, private sector, and pension fund contributions. Plan outlines his priorities for creating "millions of high-wage jobs and smoothing our transition from a defense- to a commercial-based economy." Tax credits, grants, and civilian job training for veterans. Tax incentives to encourage private investment.	**NOW**

Education

Wanted to be known as the "Education President." His "America 2000" program, introduced in April 1991, sought $200 million in funding from private sector for research on nontraditional schooling. "Choice" concept rejected by Congress on grounds that, by providing federal funds to religious schools, it violates constitutional separation of church and state.	His 1991 "Arkansas agenda" included higher taxes for education, forfeiture of driver's licenses for school dropouts. Teachers' unions unsuccessfully fought his 1983 plan for teacher testing. Sales tax rise in 1991 went to education trust fund.	**THEN**
Will ask Congress for $500 million to build 535 "New American Schools" (one per congressional district) by 1996. Voluntary testing in 4th, 8th, and 12th grade in English, math, science, history, and geography. Rewards for schools achieving national goals. Merit pay for teachers. Platform backs parents' right to choose private, public, or religious schools and supports "the right of students to engage in voluntary prayer in schools."	Double federal spending on education, aiming at inner cities and rural areas. Let college students pay off tuition loans through community service. Create apprenticeship programs for high school students not bound for college and adult education programs for those without high school diplomas. Opposes Republicans' "private school vouchers" and calls for teachers' pay that "measures up to their decisive role in children's lives."	**NOW**

BUSH and PLATFORM	CLINTON and PLATFORM

Energy/Environment

THEN	Signed Clean Air Act of 1990. In 1991 supported regulations to open millions of acres of wetlands to development. Supports logging in ancient forests though it threatens endangered spotted owl, arguing that lumber jobs take priority. In May 1992, announced he would allow industries to raise their air-pollution emissions above allowable levels specified in the Clean Air Act without giving prior notice to allow public comment. Administration argues that the delays of public-comment process cause burden on industry.	Criticized as governor for failing to clean up White River in Arkansas from poultry industry waste runoff. Defends record by saying "short-term tradeoffs between jobs and the environment...were made tougher by federal cutbacks in aid to clean up the environment...."
NOW	Stresses Clean Air Act, blames Congress for ignoring his plan to "cut our dependence on foreign oil by seven million barrels a day." Platform says "environmental progress is integrally related to economic advancement.... private ownership and economic freedom are the best security against environmental degradation."	Reduce energy consumption by at least 25%. Through new regulations, encourage utilities to invest in conservation. Stop building nuclear power plants unless safe way found to dispose of waste. Emphasize natural gas over oil and promote solar and wind power. Opposes oil drilling in Arctic Wildlife Refuge. Might support small increase in federal gasoline tax. Tax credit incentives for companies to improve waste-recovery and recycling programs. Supports national bottle bill requiring deposits on all glass and plastic bottles. Supports research to make cars more fuel-efficient. Running mate Gore wants "global Marshall Plan" as "response to the environmental crisis."

International Affairs

THEN	In his first 24 months in office, communism broke down in Eastern Europe, Germany was reunified, the Soviet Union started disintegrating, the Cold War ended. Bush led alliance that won the Gulf War and spoke of "new world order." Traveled extensively to see world leaders. Resisted demands for crackdown on China after Tiananmen massacre.	No experience in international affairs, except trade-mission trips as governor. As national politician, has generally supported Bush in foreign policy, though straddled on how he would have voted on use of force in Gulf, saying, "I guess I would have voted with the majority if it was a close vote. But I agree with the argument the minority made."

Issues: Gun Control, Health Care

BUSH and PLATFORM	CLINTON and PLATFORM	
Takes credit ("I saw a chance to help, and I did") for collapse of communism in eastern Europe and former Soviet Union: "the Cold War is over, and freedom finished first." Stresses need for America to lead post-Cold War world. Has improved relations with new Israeli government after blocking loan guarantees over settlement policy dispute.	Argues that United States must remain a world leader. Says he supported President Bush's intervention in Iraq but criticizes the President for being slow to respond to events in Russia and for not imposing trade sanctions on China. Opposes Israeli settlements in the West Bank, but says that they should not stop immigration aid to Israel.	**NOW**

Gun Control

Opposed mandatory waiting period for people to purchase a hand gun.	As governor, signed bill supported by National Rifle Association making harassment of hunters a crime. Vetoed NRA-backed measure that would have prevented local governments from regulating guns.	**THEN**
Backed waiting period for gun purchase if proposal were in crime bill he approved; crime bill was still in Congress when campaign began. Platform defends "constitutional right to keep and bear arms. We call for stiff mandatory sentences for those who use firearms in a crime."	Favors stalled crime bill's requirement for a five- or seven-day waiting period before a firearm purchase. Platform calls for "controls to ban the possession, sale, importation, and manufacture of the most deadly assault weapons."	**NOW**

Health Care

1990: "I am committed to bring the staggering costs of health care under control." 1992: proposed a health insurance tax credit of up to $3,750 to help low-income families afford health insurance. Introduced "Healthy Start," a program of prenatal and infant health care and immunization.	As governor, started health clinics in schools, where condoms are distributed. He has fought to improve Arkansas's dismal health record: high child death rate, underweight-baby rate. 1 in 4 Arkansans has no health insurance, compared to 1 in 7 nationally.	**THEN**
Opposes national health insurance. Wants to preserve the public-private health care system through comprehensive reforms. Health care should not lead to government controls or rationing, require new spending by states or employers, require a tax increase, or threaten older Americans	"Putting People First" program says affordable, quality health care will be a right, not a privilege. Says no tax increase would be required. Promises move to radically control costs by changing incentives, reducing paperwork, and cracking down on drug and insurance	**NOW**

BUSH and PLATFORM	CLINTON and PLATFORM

NOW

Health Care continued
with benefit cuts or premium increases. Bush would give the poor vouchers, $1,250 for an individual and $3,750 a year for a family; the middle class would get similar subsidies in the form of tax deductions. Puts "health care choices... in the hands of the people, not government bureaucrats." AIDS "should be treated like any other communicable or sexually transmitted disease, while at the same time preserving patient confidentiality." Attacks Clinton health plan as "a new payroll tax for a government takeover of health care."

company fraud. Would require employers to provide private insurance coverage for workers or pay an additional tax into public fund to cover uninsured. All businesses, regardless of size, would pay set amount per employee. Government board would regulate and standardize medical-care prices, set national and state spending caps, and regulate spread of medical technology. He would then phase in guaranteed universal access to basic medical insurance coverage as prices drop. Supports more AIDS research and more services to the elderly.

Taxes

THEN

In 1988 presidential campaign: "Read my lips: no new taxes!" In March 1992 vetoed bill targeted to middle class even though bill included six of Bush's seven tax-cut proposals. Objected to new, higher (36%) tax bracket for $115,000 individuals and $140,000 couples and a 10% surtax on millionaires. Proposal included $500 increase in personal exemption for dependent children; student loan interest deduction; $5,000 credit, no penalty IRA withdrawal for first-time home buyers.

Earlier in campaign, supported a tax cut and a children's tax credit for middle-class taxpayers. Later, he proposed to offer taxpayers the choice of either an increased credit for each child or a larger tax reduction. GOP says he raised "taxes and fees 128 times" as governor, but tax reductions were not counted. Arkansas is 49th in state rankings of per capita state and local taxes.

NOW

Promises across-the-board tax cuts tied to cuts in spending. Would give taxpayers right to check box on tax returns to earmark 10% of tax payment to deficit reduction. Would decrease capital gains tax from 28% to 15.4% to encourage investment and would repeal luxury tax on yachts. Would give 10% tax credit, up to $5,000, on certain home purchases. Will "continue to fight to increase the personal exemption." Platform: "only safeguard" against Democratic tax increases "is the use of the veto by George Bush and enough Republican votes in Congress to sustain it....The proper path to create jobs

Would cut income taxes of most Americans by 10% and offset cost with higher taxes on those with incomes above $200,000. Replace current $2,100 dependent exemption with tax credit of $800 per child. Cut capital gains tax for investments held at least five years in new businesses. Give investment tax credits to small and medium-sized businesses. Prohibit businesses from writing off cost of excessive salaries and bonuses for executives. Middle-class taxpayers will have a choice between children's tax credit or significant reduction in their income tax rate. No more tax breaks for

BUSH and PLATFORM	CLINTON and PLATFORM	
and growth is tax rate reductions." His tax-cut message in acceptance speech was not accompanied by details on how he would specifically cut spending to make up for lost revenue.	companies that shut down American plants to move overseas. Crack down on non-U.S. companies manipulating tax laws to their advantage. Platform: "We will relieve the tax burden on middle-class Americans by forcing the rich to pay their fair share."	**N O W**

Trade

Has worked to remove restrictions on U.S. goods being sold overseas. Has asked Japan to buy more American goods.	While chairman of National Governors Association backed report emphasizing competitiveness and more language instruction in schools and joint multi-state trade missions.	**T H E N**
Negotiated comprehensive plan for U.S.-Canadian-Mexican free-trade agreement. Supports trade deal with Mexico that includes safeguards protecting environment and American jobs and industries.	Favors Mexican free-trade agreement but would require stricter environmental and labor standards in Mexico. Says he is basically a free-trader but supports retaliation if Japan keeps out American products. Would create Economic Security Council, similar in status to National Security Council, with responsibility for coordinating America's international economic policy.	**N O W**

Welfare

Increased funding for Head Start. Opposed bills to extend unemployment benefits with borrowed money until Congress found the money (from collection of estimated taxes).	As governor, initiated an experimental program in which welfare recipients learned how to look for a job in exchange for benefits. As National Governors Association chairman was a proponent of federal welfare reform.	**T H E N**
Promises to "strike a new course" and "overhaul the engine" of social services. Emphasizes need to build moral and family values of people on welfare. Supports experiments in welfare approaches by states through exemptions from federal laws. Distrusts welfare bureaucrats, saying "when it comes to raising children, government doesn't know best, parents know best."	Provide training and child care but in most instances require an adult, after two years on welfare, to take a private or public service job or lose benefits. In some cases, allow people to stay on welfare more than two years if they are making progress in education programs. Vague about what he would provide for children if their parents refused to work.	**N O W**

MAPPING

THE

STRATEGY

THEY WAVED AND THEY GRINNED and they set off—Clinton and Gore on their bus heading out of New York City toward the heartland, Bush and Quayle flying out of Houston to the South. Wherever their campaign journey began, the candidates followed a compass pointing them and their issues toward the goal of 270 electoral votes, the number needed to win the presidency. They offered broad themes: "trust me" from Bush, "change things" from Clinton. They also tailored issues to fit. Clinton in industrial states never let voters forget the recession, and Bush in the conservative South sternly noted that God was not mentioned in the Democratic platform.

The President needed to say more than just put your trust in God and George Bush. So he proclaimed family values, a theme that neatly fitted into his promise of trust. He also needed to show how his strength in international affairs could help the faltering U.S. economy. And, thanks to his friend and adviser Jim Baker, Bush found a way.

Baker, switching from Secretary of State to campaign boss, spelled out the theme in his farewell speech to the State Department: "The President knows that all policies have to be brought together....We must concentrate on the interrelationship between domestic and foreign policy, and between economic and security policy."

Suddenly, there was a vision, though it used a rearview mirror: look back at the first term and you see Bush at work ending the Cold War; now look ahead and see this trusted President solving the nation's domestic problems in his second term. Baker, formerly Secretary of the Treasury and President Reagan's Chief of Staff, personified the synergism between national and international affairs.

Only the President, said Bush campaign manager Fred Malek, can "put in context what has taken place in the world over the past 12 years and what America's role has been in reshaping the world, and what this has meant not only to the world, but what it has meant to Americans here at home. How it has improved our prospects for the future in terms of the peace dividend, export opportunities, and the like."

Bush, in his acceptance speech, hit Clinton hard for his lack of experience in international affairs. Bush, recalling how he mustered the forces that drove Saddam Hussein out of Kuwait, said, "Well, what about the leader of the Arkansas National Guard, the man who hopes to be commander-in-chief? Well, I bit the bullet and he bit his nails. And two days—listen to this now—two days after Congress voted to follow my lead, my opponent said this, and I quote directly, 'I guess I would have voted with the majority if it was a close vote. But I agree with the argument the minority made.'"

Bush's criticism of Clinton's lack of experience did not seem to be an issue with the voters. A CNN/USA *Today*/Gallup poll in late August showed that 78 percent of the voters surveyed did not doubt Clinton's ability to serve as commander-in-chief. Another, earlier poll had a vast majority of voters saying they thought Bush could handle international affairs better than Clinton, who got only 21 percent on that question. But, asked to rate issues they want to hear the candidates discuss, voters rated the domestic economy high above international policy.

That was the risk. How could Bush talk about the economy? As Clinton continually reminded voters, under Bush the United States had had the

Electoral Map of the United States

WA. 11
OR. 7
ID. 4
MT. 3
WY. 3
N. D. 3
S. D. 3
NE. 5
NV. 4
UT. 5
CO. 8
CA. 54
AZ. 8
N.M. 5
KS. 6
OK. 8
TX. 32
MN. 10
IA. 7
MO. 11
AR. 6
LA. 9
WI. 11
IL. 22
MS. 7
MI. 18
IN. 12
KY. 8
TN. 11
AL. 9
GA. 13
OH. 21
W.V. 5
VA. 13
N.C. 14
S.C. 8
FL. 25
PA. 23
N.Y. 33
N.H. 4
VT. 3
ME. 4
MA. 12
R.I. 4
CT. 8
N.J. 15
DE. 3
MD. 10
D.C. 3
AK. 3
HI. 4

To win the election, a candidate must get a majority of electoral votes: 270. Electoral votes in some states have changed since 1988 because the 1990 census revealed population shifts that mandated congressional redistricting. Ross Perot's withdrawal lessened the chance that the election would be decided in the House of Representatives. But Perot's name remains on the ballot in most states.

lowest economic growth rate, the worst job-growth rate, the lowest income growth rate, and the lowest industrial production rate since World War II. Unemployment had risen from 5.4 percent when he was sworn in as President to 7.7 percent when he was renominated. There had been 19,540,000 manufacturing jobs at the beginning of his first term, and as he sought a second term there were 18,210,000. Average hourly earnings in 1982 dollars had dropped from $7.68 to $7.45, housing starts from 1,620,000 to 1,120,000. Inflation was down and exports were up, but those were the only glimmers in a dark economy.

Clinton's agent-of-change theme had never appealed to Bush campaign strategists, though Bush used the word whenever he could. "The voters' natural instinct," Bush pollster Fred Steeper remarked, "would be to make a change because they perceive things to be lousy." So the Republicans decided to "make the case that Clinton will make things worse."

The commander-in-chief campaigns before American Legionnaires.

The Republican theme, then, came down to, look at Clinton and look at Bush; look at our values and our experience—and make your choice. The strategy started to work immediately. Bush went into the convention with polls that showed voters picking Clinton over Bush by 17 percent. Bush came out of the convention with the gap narrowed to 45 for Clinton, 42 for Bush; the margin of error made the race neck-and-neck. But a CNN/*USA Today* poll conducted a week after the convention showed Clinton leading Bush, 52 to 42.

As a secondary theme, Bush reached back to an idea first circulated in the spring of 1991, when House Republican whip Newt Gingrich of Georgia urged the President to battle Congress in Harry Truman style. "If [Bush] wants to be an effective President in his second term," Gingrich said at the time, "he has to get working control of the Congress." In 1948, an underdog Truman, fighting what he called "the do-nothing" Republican Congress, won an upset victory over Thomas E. Dewey and carried on his coattails 75 new Democratic House members and 9 Senators. This gave the Democrats majorities in both houses.

Bush, in his acceptance speech, identified himself as another Harry Truman, taking Truman's 1948 words as his own: "This is more than a political call to arms. Give me your help, not to win votes alone, but to win this new crusade and keep America safe and secure for its own people."

While Bush urges the voters to "Clean the House" and give him a

Republican Congress, history shows that in the past 60 years, the Republicans have had control of both the presidency and Congress for only two years during the Eisenhower Administration. Bush's war on Congress, attractive to conservatives like Gingrich, may have another effect: a broadening of support for Clinton by Democrats lower on the ticket. Instead of a Bush-Clinton contest, it would be a Bush-Congress battle. The strategy had much more attraction for Republican congressional candidates when Bush was achieving high approval ratings.

L inked strategically with spreading the word on issues was spreading money and time where they presumably would do the most good. Republicans and Democrats focused their resources on what strategists call "The Lock"—the Republicans' longtime hold on the Electoral College. In each of the last three elections, Republican victories have always included 38 states whose electoral votes total 408. An essential key to the lock has been California, which Republicans have carried in nine of the last ten elections; only Barry Goldwater lost it in Lyndon B. Johnson's 1964 landslide. This year, however, Republicans cannot be certain of victory in California, where unemployment is high and the state government, gridlocked over a budget deficit, was for a time paying bills with IOUs.

California, immense and diverse, is a costly advertising arena. Both Democrats and Republicans must decide how much to spend there, especially on television. Democrats can take a chance on holding down spending because polls show the state leaning strongly toward Clinton. Less advertising in California means that more money can go for campaigning in other vital states. But, in a close election, being stingy in California might cost the Democrats the state—and the election. Republicans must also decide whether to pour money into a state they may very well lose.

Bush has no questions about where his biggest effort must be made: the five major industrial states—New Jersey, Pennsylvania, Ohio, Michigan, and Illinois. They have a total of 99 electoral votes. If Bush can take three of these states, he can absorb the loss of California, with its 54 electoral votes, and anticipated Clinton victories in the South.

Although the five states are plagued by unemployment, Bush takes a chance in giving them an economic message. All he can say basically is that Clinton would only make things worse. The Republicans claim that Democratic economic programs always come down to "tax and spend" and that Clinton's economic program, which calls for $150 billion in tax

Six Views of Democracy In America

In the maternity ward of a Detroit hospital, a CNN camera focuses on a black baby, and the viewer learns about the human reality behind a political issue: The black baby is more than twice as likely as a white infant to die in its first year, three and a half times as likely to grow up without a father in the home. A black male baby who lives to his teens is seven times more likely to be murdered than a white teenager.

A businessman talks about health care. He had an employee who had to quit because of medical problems. She had no health insurance and had to go on welfare. "So," the businessman says, "in reality, I'm paying for it right now." She is one of the statistics, one of the millions, made into an individual by CNN's six-hour "Democracy in America" series.

The first three programs, collectively called "The Nation's Agenda," look at issues challenging what once was known as the American Dream: an urban underclass, the ills of our industry and work force, the gridlock of government. The second set of programs—their theme, "The Battle to Lead"—examines the record, character, and leadership of President Bush and Vice President Quayle and their challengers, Bill Clinton and Al Gore.

The series, part of CNN's "Democracy in America" coverage, will be anchored by Bernard Shaw, CNN's principal Washington anchor. The programs have been funded with the assistance of the Markle Foundation, following a study of the 1988 election by its Commission on the Media and the Electorate. The study recommended expanded uses of broadcasting to provide a remedy for what it called "the dangerous disconnect between voters and their own electoral process." The foundation's funding of the CNN series is a result of that recommendation. The programs are produced by CNN's Special Assignment Unit under the direction of Pamela Hill, vice president and executive producer, in cooperation with the CNN Political Unit and its director Tom Hannon.

The series will be broadcast from 10 to 11 p.m., Eastern Time.

Sunday, Sept. 20

THE NATION'S AGENDA: A HOUSE DIVIDED

What is the cost of healing the wounds of the inner city? Can the whites of the suburbs and the blacks of mean streets ever be brought together? "There was a time in America," Bernard Shaw begins, "when the struggle for racial justice seemed simple, a battle between good and evil. There was a time when there were villains and victims, a time of moral certainty." Today black children gun each other down in our schools and on our streets. Villain and victim have the same address. The correspondents on "A House Divided" are Norma Quarles and Kathy Slobogin.

Sunday, Sept. 27

THE NATION'S AGENDA: THE PILLARS OF OUR PROSPERITY

"It's been a pretty bad year," says one of the statistics who is part of the nation's reported 7.7 percent unemployed. "Very stressful and then losing my job. I've done the best I could, you know, with the economy the way it is." The national debt totals nearly $4 trillion. This year alone the interest payments on the debt will come to nearly $1,000 for every man, woman, and child in America. CNN Correspondent Frank Sesno, with Senior Producer Steve Singer, translate the numbers into human faces and voices.

Sunday, Oct. 4

THE NATION'S AGENDA: A GOVERNMENT FOR THE PEOPLE

Pete Simmons, senior producer, calls it "government gridlock, a bureaucratic tangle." CNN Special Assignment Correspondent Brooks Jackson plunges into the tangle to find out what happens to a critical issue—health care—when, as Simmons says, "special interests, divided government, and bureaucratic inertia whipsaw it in every self-serving direction." The program shows government and lobbyists at work. "We know about the presidential veto," a Washington insider says, "but what we have on health care and other issues is the money veto." Washington has become so bad, Jackson points out, that even some of the politicians are leaving.

Sunday, Oct. 11

THE BATTLE TO LEAD: A HEARTBEAT AWAY

"Five of our last nine Presidents served as Vice President," says Andrew Schlesinger, co-producer, of this look at the running mates of President Bush and Bill Clinton. Our first Vice President, John Adams, defined the dual reality of his role: "In this I am nothing, but I may be everything." Schlesinger produces the Dan Quayle section of the program, with CNN anchor Catherine Crier. Mary Whittington is producer of the Al Gore section, with John Camp as correspondent.

Sunday, Oct. 18

THE BATTLE TO LEAD: BILL CLINTON OF ARKANSAS

A look at the five-term governor of Arkansas "from the vantage point of the state's changing educational, economic, and environmental health," says producer Richard Cohen. Correspondent Ken Bode assesses Clinton's leadership in Arkansas and forecasts what to expect of him if he becomes President.

Sunday, Oct. 25

THE BATTLE TO LEAD: THE PUBLIC MIND OF GEORGE BUSH

A meticulous examination of the President on five issues. Civil rights: why he has twisted and turned on civil rights legislation. An examination of his record from the 1964 Civil Rights Act to the Los Angeles riots. Abortion: following a trail from supporter of population control to opponent—and then advocate of a constitutional amendment to ban abortion. China: Bush's special country, ruled by leaders he long has known. Oil: the man whose offshore equipment company drilled the first oil wells in Kuwaiti waters; a 40-year knowledge of the oil business. Leadership: how he has handled education, the economy, and the environment—and how he has dealt with leaders of former communist nations. Ken Bode is correspondent and Jim Connor and Jane Stone are co-producers.

The "Democracy in America" coverage also features reports on campaign financing ("Who Pays") and negative and misleading advertising ("Ad Police") by Special Assignment Correspondent Brooks Jackson. Other "Democracy in America" specials and investigative reports will be aired during the campaign.

The Markle Foundation also supplies funds to the nonprofit, nonpartisan Center for National Independence in Politics, which provides objective information on gubernatorial and congressional candidates. By calling the center's Voter Information Hotline (1-800-786-6885) people can ask an operator questions about a candidate. For printed information, call 1-900-786-6885 (cost $3.50) for the biographies, finances, voting records, and issue positions of specific candidates.

increases over the next four years, actually will cost $500 billion.

In these battleground states, Clinton's message encompasses health care, education, and the economy. The middle class has been suffering, he tells rallies, because the "country has been in the grip of a false economic theory." He describes the Republican doctrine as simply keeping taxes low for the wealthy. "It hasn't worked," he says. "I want to replace trickle-down economics with people-first economics." Clinton communications director George Stephanopoulos calls the message a "web issue"—the opposite of a "wedge issue," because it unites voters from varied racial, economic, and regional bases.

Bush expects strong Republican efforts in the three states that have GOP governors—Ohio, Illinois, and Michigan. New Jersey's Democratic governor, James J. Florio, is viewed by Republicans as an asset, too, because tax increases during his administration have lost much voter support. Pennsylvania's Democratic governor, Robert P. Casey, is also unpopular for the same reason. Casey, who was denied the chance to speak out against abortion at the Democratic convention, is cool toward Clinton and his abortion-rights stand. Bush's anti-abortion, family-value campaigning in these five states is aimed particularly at their large Roman Catholic populations. Bush also stresses his "school-choice" proposal, which would give parents vouchers good for paying tuition in private or religious schools. Bush's choice plan, opposed by Clinton, appeals to Catholic parents of parochial school pupils. Catholics, says Bush campaign chairman Robert M. Teeter, "have been an important part of the Reagan/Bush coalition, and they are very important to us this year."

Republicans also warn that Clinton's defense cuts would add more workers to already long unemployment rolls and that Clinton's running

Debate Schedule

Three presidential debates and one vice presidential debate are tentatively scheduled during the campaign. Each of the 90-minute debates will start at 9 p.m., Eastern Time. The proposed dates are:

Presidential debates:	Tuesday, September 22
	Sunday, October 4
	Thursday, October 15
Vice presidential debate:	Tuesday, September 29

Clinton and Gore launch their campaign with a bus trip.

mate, Al Gore, is guilty of "environmental extremism." The imposition of stringent fuel standards for autos, say Republicans, would raise sticker prices and slow down purchases, meaning more layoffs in Michigan and Ohio.

In 1988, Democratic candidate Michael Dukakis won only 10 states and the District of Columbia, collecting 112 electoral votes. Bush took 40 states and their 426 electoral votes. But beneath the surface of this seemingly lopsided victory were some numbers that intrigue strategists this year. Dukakis, regarded as a far weaker campaigner than Clinton, was much stronger than Mondale in 1984, Carter in 1980, McGovern in 1972, and Humphrey in 1968. Clinton would not have to do much better than Dukakis in some states, such as Michigan and Pennsylvania, to rack up enough electoral votes to beat Bush.

The fight will be ferocious. Peggy Noonan, who worked in the Reagan White House and wrote Bush's read-my-lips line, forecasts "one of the great campaigns, a bruising contest." When politics gets this tough, she said, "a wonderful thing happens, as if by accident. The talk turns to serious questions, they argue over serious issues, over different ways of seeing the world and how the American people ought to go about their pursuit of happiness. We're all going to remember this one. Keep the kids up—they're going to see democracy in one of its great barbaric yawps."

Acknowledgments

The author wishes to thank the following people for their help: Tom Johnson, president of CNN; Ed Turner, executive vice president of CNN; Tom Hannon; Susan Steele; Craig Leachman; Annie Harris; Estelle Tarica; Fred Bracken; Susan Tungate; Jennifer Falk Weiss; my wife, Scottie; and Bob Shogan, who has covered politics almost as long as he has been my friend. Turner Publishing would like to acknowledge: Bill Burke, Kathy Christensen, Terry Davila, David Greenspan, Barbara Griffin, Cecilia Harrington, Laura Heald, Lori Jones, Peri Koch, Larry Larson, Vivian Lawand, Rhonda Myers, Virginia Pirie, Kevin Smith, Paul Van den bossche, Tammy Winter, Ann Williams.